KU-313-395

Miller

THE PLAYWRIGHT

by

DENNIS WELLAND

METHUEN · LONDON AND NEW YORK

First published in Great Britain in 1979 in simultaneous hardback and paperback editions by Eyre Methuen Ltd
Second, revised and expanded edition published as a Methuen Paperback in 1983 in London by Methuen London Ltd, 11 New Fetter Lane, London EC4P 4EE and in USA by Methuen Inc, 733 Third Avenue, New York NY10017.

Copyright © 1979, 1983 by Dennis Welland

ISBN 0 413 521109 (Paperback)

Printed in Great Britain by Redwood Burn Ltd.
Trowbridge, Wiltshire

KING ALFRED'S COLLEGE
WINCHESTER.

812.5
MIL

97575

This paperback edition is sold subject to the condition that it shall not, by way of trade or otherwise, be lent, resold, hired out, or otherwise circulated without the publisher's prior consent in any form of binding or cover other than that in which it is published and without a similar condition including this condition being imposed on the subsequent purchaser.

Contents

Illustrations

Author's Note

As the reader may have encountered one or both of my earlier books on Arthur Miller an explanation of the relationship between them and the present volume may be in order. The earliest, *Arthur Miller*, had the distinction, on its publication in 1961, of being the first book-length study of Miller to appear anywhere. The nature of the series for which it was written (Oliver & Boyd's 'Writers and Critics') reinforced my own wish at that time to treat Miller as a man of letters and not exclusively as a dramatist. I have not changed my belief that it is helpful to see his work as a whole and in the perspective of a tradition of American literature going back at least as far as Emerson: this will be apparent at a number of places in the chapters that follow, but with less emphasis than in 1961. Some of my views on Miller's earlier work have, not unnaturally, changed with the passage of time, but many remain substantially the same. Indeed, so many of my 1961 comments and speculations have been confirmed by what Miller has written since that it would be pointless to vary them for the sake of novelty.

By 1978, however, the Miller canon had grown considerably and critical comment on all aspects of that canon had proliferated. He had written, in the interim, a film-script, a television script, at least seven more plays, and a number of prose works of various kinds. It seemed a suitable time to revise and up-date my own work on him, and in 1979 I brought out *Miller: A Study of His Plays* in Methuen's 'Modern Theatre Profiles' series. The growth of the Miller canon and again the nature of the series led me this time to concentrate on Miller as a dramatist and on the plays as pieces for theatrical presentation. It still seemed desirable to regard Miller's career as beginning in 1944 with the New York production of *The Man Who Had All the Luck* and to leave out of account the plays he wrote as an undergraduate and those written later for radio, so as to focus more sharply on his best-known dramas, the texts of which are more readily accessible.

In the Author's Note to that volume I expressed the cautious belief that 'his reputation, though secure, is probably rather less high now than it was [in 1961]'. I could not, when writing that, foresee the success that would be enjoyed by the National Theatre's London revival of *Death of A Salesman* later in 1979 with Warren Mitchell as Willy Loman, nor the revivals of other plays (in particular *The Crucible*) on both sides of the Atlantic and, in the case of *After the Fall* at least, in Hong Kong. In the summer of 1979 came the controversial announcement of the choice of Vanessa Redgrave for the principal role in *Playing For Time*, his powerful television play about Auschwitz that was screened, to great acclaim, in 1980. Also in 1980 *The American Clock* was first staged in the United States and its first British production is scheduled for April 1983 at the Birmingham Repertory Theatre. All this, together with the demand for *Miller: A Study of His Plays*, led to the revision, expansion and up-dating of that book which the present volume represents. One wholly new chapter is included here (Chapter 12), others have been slightly altered in places in the light of material now available, and of course the critical apparatus has been brought as far as possible up to date. In short, *Miller the Playwright* supersedes *Miller: A Study of His Plays* and *Arthur Miller* only in respect of the ground that it covers and the up-to-date accuracy of its information.

At pages 9 to 11 inclusive a Chronological Table lists briefly the main events in Miller's life of which the reader may wish to be reminded as a framework for the discussion that follows. It notes the first publication of his books and the first production of each of his plays. At pages 164 to 168 inclusive will be found a fuller tabulation of 'American and British Premieres of Miller's Plays and Films', and at page 169 this is followed by a 'Bibliographical Note'. These are intended to support the text and should not be thought of as exhaustive. No attempt is made to record productions of the plays elsewhere in the world or revivals. Similarly the 'Bibliographical Note' lists only the publications in book form, confident that the reader who so wishes may be directed by those books towards the large body of essays biographical and critical that grows steadily. The Notes (at pages 158 to 163) I have endeavoured to keep as brief as possible, restricting them for the most part, though by no means exclusively, to the provision of finding-references and acknowledgments.

Arthur Miller

1915 Born in Manhattan, New York City, 17 October, second son of Isadore and Augusta Miller.

1929 Isadore Miller's clothing business being adversely affected by the Depression, the family moves to Brooklyn.

1932 Graduates from High School and works in automobile-parts warehouse for $15 a week (cf. Bert in *A Memory of Two Mondays*).

1934 Enters University of Michigan, Ann Arbor.

1936 *Honors at Dawn* produced at Ann Arbor and wins the Avery Hopwood Drama Award ($250).

1937 *They Too Arise* (originally entitled *No Villain*) produced at Ann Arbor and also wins Avery Hopwood Award and the Theatre Guild Bureau of New Plays prize.

1938 Receives degree of B.A., University of Michigan.
      Begins work with Federal Theatre Project.

1940 Marries Mary Slattery.

1944 Visits army camps for material for film script *The Story of G.I. Joe*.
      Situation Normal (prose account of this tour) published.
      The Man Who Had All the Luck produced in New York and wins Theatre Guild National Prize.

1945 *Focus* (a novel) published.

1947 *All My Sons* produced in New York and wins the New York Drama Critics' Circle Award.

1949 *Death of a Salesman* produced in New York; wins New York Drama Critics' Circle Award and Pulitzer Prize.

1950 *An Enemy of the People* (an adaptation of Ibsen's play) produced in New York.

1953 *The Crucible* produced in New York and wins the Antoinette Perry and the Donaldson Prizes.

1954 Is refused passport by the State Department to attend Brussels opening of *The Crucible* in March.
'A Modest Proposal for the Pacification of the Public Temper' (satirical political essay) in *The Nation* 3 July.

1955 'The American Theatre' and 'A Boy grew in Brooklyn' published in *Holiday*, January and March respectively. *A Memory of Two Mondays* and *A View from the Bridge* produced in New York as a double bill.
Commissioned by New York City Youth Board to write a film-script on street gangs, but the Board delays ratification and, in December, cancels the project because of rumours of an impending political investigation of Miller.

1956 Two-act version of *A View from the Bridge* produced in London.
'The Family in Modern Drama' published in *Atlantic*, April.
Divorce ends marriage to Mary Slattery in June.
Receives honorary doctorate at University of Michigan 16 June.
Appears before House Un-American Activities Committee 21 June.
Marries Marilyn Monroe 29 June.
Passport renewed for six months (instead of normal two years) in July.

1957 Convicted of contempt of Congress for refusing to name suspected communists 31 May. No penalty imposed.
'The Misfits' (short story) published in *Esquire*, October.
Collected Plays published.

1958 '*Death of a Salesman* : a Symposium' published in the *Tulane Drama Review*, May.
'The Shadows of the Gods: a critical view of the American Theater' in *Harper's Magazine*, August.
Conviction for contempt of Congress unanimously reversed by the Supreme Court in August.
Elected to the National Arts and Letters Institute.

1959 Receives honorary degree from the Hebrew University of Jerusalem.
Awarded the Gold Medal for Drama by the National Arts and Letters Institute.

1960 Filming of *The Misfits* takes place in Nevada from August to November.
Separates from Marilyn Monroe in November.

1961 Divorced by Marilyn Monroe 20 January.
Film of *The Misfits* released.
The Misfits published as a novel.

1962 Marries Austrian-born photographer Ingeborg Morath.
Death of Marilyn Monroe.

1963 Publishes *Jane's Blanket*, a children's book.

1964 *After the Fall* produced in New York.
Incident at Vichy produced in New York.

1965 Elected International President of P.E.N., until 1969.

1967 *I Don't Need You Any More* (short stories) published.

1968 *The Price* produced in New York.

1969 Directs London production of *The Price*.
Receives Brandeis University Creative Arts award.
In Russia published with Inge Morath.

1970 *Fame* produced in New York.

1972 *The Creation of the World, and Other Business* produced in New York.

1974 *Up from Paradise* produced at Ann Arbor, Michigan.
Miller directs and plays the Narrator.

1977 *The Archbishop's Ceiling* produced in Washington, D.C.
In the Country published with Inge Morath.

1978 Visits China with Inge Morath.
Fame presented on television.
The Theater Essays of Arthur Miller published.

1979 *Chinese Encounters* published with Inge Morath.

1980 *The American Clock* produced in New York.
Playing for Time presented on television.

I
Introduction

It is more than thirty years since the first production of *Death of a Salesman*. To many people this comes as a surprise and the play's prescription in English schools as a text for the A-level examination may seem the kiss of death for its status as contemporary and innovatory. To others the number and extent of the changes that the theatre has seen internationally since 1949 will seem to have left Miller stranded in his dedication to what now appear more conventional dramatic forms. In any definitive and balanced study of twentieth-century drama in the English language, however, Miller will always occupy a position of significance, whatever further plays he may or may not write.

By the historically-minded he will be respected for having dramatised the mood of post-war America with particular vividness and insight, but his plays are much more than the socio-political documents of the age to which some discussion has tended to reduce them. Less prolific as a playwright than either Eugene O'Neill or Tennessee Williams, he is less repetitive than either of them in subject-matter and in dramatic form. That his experiments have not all been equally felicitous is less important than his achievement as a whole and the directions into which he has tried to steer the drama. The most socially conscious of all major American dramatists, he has always taken a stance more moral than strictly political and focused on issues human rather than ideological. This has irritated some critics, but will help keep the plays from dating. He is a concerned dramatist, rather than a committed one; a thinking writer rather than the intellectual that he has often been called.

(2)

Of Miller's stage plays only three—*A Memory of Two Mondays*, *Incident at Vichy,* and *The Archbishop's Ceiling* — do not deal primarily with family tensions. His treatment of the family avoids the sentimentality of Thornton Wilder's, the claustrophobic intensity of O'Neill's or Williams's, or the more tortured and contemptuous attitude of Edward Albee, largely because he relates the frictions of family life to those of the macrocosm outside: his families live in a recognisably real world. That this is not fortuitous can be seen from his two critical essays written while he was working on *A View from the Bridge,* the play where the family and society interact most crucially.[1] These make it clear that he has no interest in family plays merely as a means of delineating the affectional ties that link us to our relatives : 'Sentimentalism is perfectly all right, but it is nowhere near a great challenge, and to pursue it . . . is not going to bring us closer to the fated mission of the drama'. Drama ought 'to bring us closer to ourselves if only it can grow and change with the changing world'. The question it asks is 'How may a man make for himself a home in that vastness of strangers and how may he transform that vastness into a home?' For Miller, as for Eliot, although in a different way, 'Home is where one starts from'. It is not the responsibility of the dramatist to draw up blue-prints for a new society, but to give the news of the present : it is the drama's 'capacity to open up the present' that Miller stresses in these essays, and one aspect of the present on which his plays insist is the impact of the public life on the private. In 'laying siege to the fortress of unrelatedness,' his drama constantly sees the family as one of the ways in which the individual is related to society; if it is often a threat to his individuality, it can also be sometimes a means by which that individuality acquires a fortifying solidarity with others.

(3)

To the critic Miller's readiness to theorise about his dramatic practice can be a useful stimulus — sometimes to disagreement. To the producer it may be an irritant, and one of them has complained of 'his impulse to expatiate to the acting company too elaborately, sometimes too intellectually, on the motivations of his writing'.[2] One of Miller's speculations in 'The Family in Modern Drama', however, must be faced at once : 'It is true to say, I think, that the language of the family is the language of the private life — prose. The language of society, the language of the public life, is verse'. The implications of this will be considered in the context of those plays to which it has most relevance; that he should have made the observation at all, however, in a country where the disjunction between verse and drama has been almost total, is indicative of another of his peculiar merits, and one that becomes unexpectedly prominent with the passing of time.

Language is one aspect of the theatre that has undergone changes remarkably radical since the Second World War. Permissiveness has been only one factor contributing to its shift away from the central position that the spoken word has traditionally held in drama. When Miller's dramas were first attracting attention in England it was a familiar criticism that, like Eugene O'Neill, he could not give language the kind of lift that was felt to be theatrically essential. It would have seemed perverse to foresee a time when a command of language would be advanced as one of Miller's claims on our respect, yet changing perspectives now seem to justify it.

When *Death of a Salesman* opened in London in July 1949 John Gielgud was starring only a few hundred yards away in *The Lady's Not for Burning*. Within a month *The Cocktail Party* had its premiere at the Edinburgh Festival and six months later came the premiere of *Venus Observed* with Laurence Olivier. When the London stage was luxuriating in this riot of imagery and echoing Fry's Mendip — 'What a wonderful thing is metaphor!' — it is perhaps surprising that Miller's more quotidian language even gained a hearing.

One review of *Death of a Salesman* entitled 'Poetry without Words' saw the play as 'an attempt to make a poetic approach to everyday life without using poetry — or even heightened speech. The characters are to remain as inarticulate as they are in real life . . . the production, in short, is expected to do most of the work of evoking the heightened mood'. Though conceding that 'this play, episodic and rambling as it is, has a certain power . . . creates a world and takes us in it' and though paying generous tribute to Kazan's brilliance of production, it concluded that nothing is 'an adequate substitute for the words which just aren't there'. I recall myself and a colleague sharing this disappointment with the play's language at a good provincial repertory production in December 1950. Miller himself was subsequently to counter such criticism by saying of Willy 'that he had not the intellectual fluency to verbalize his situation is not the same thing as saying that he lacked awareness'.[3] At the time, however, British audiences were

14

more susceptible to the opposite argument as formulated by the poet-dramatist Ronald Duncan : 'it is the function of the theatre to express, not merely what a character would say in a given situation, but what he might say if he were given a poet's power of expression. For the danger, if we are not able to express our inmost feelings, is that we may very probably in time cease to feel them'.

Tone-deafened by verse-drama and familiar with strictures on the inadequacies of the American language in the theatre of Eugene O'Neill, we did not immediately recognize the range and subtleties of Miller's effects, but we were not alone in that. Even in American criticism the sensitive use of colloquial idiom and speech rhythm for literary effect had not yet been dignified with the title of 'the vernacular tradition'. Indeed, Harold Hobson recalled that 'the glittering Mr [George Jean] Nathan' had faulted the play 'on the ground of its ordinary speech, in which he saw no tragic grandeur'. Hobson's 1949 review thought it a play 'of enormous distinction' but made no special point of the language. By 1953, however, he was speaking of it as 'beautifully and movingly written, eloquent, yet perfectly within the common American idiom'. He praised particularly the tenderness of the 'Requiem' and its rhythm, and remarked that 'not many dramatists have written speeches that drive harder at the heart, or are more memorable' than Linda's 'attention must be paid' speech.

By 1954 Kenneth Tynan was calling the play 'Miller's triumph in the plain style; it rings with phrases which have entered into the contemporary subconscious'. The English poetic revival, he suggested, seemed hollow and retrogressive in comparison with the 'craggy candour' of Miller's dramatic prose. That revival has now receded so far that a British reviewer in 1968 could complain of *The Price* that its dialogue 'doesn't seem to be as eloquently contemporary as *Salesman's* was in its time, nor as sharply economical'. Those qualities were there, but were certainly not fully recognised in 1949.[4]

In the introduction to *Collected Plays* in 1957 Miller was unusually non-committal on the question, saying, perhaps with O'Neill in mind, 'We have had more than one extraordinary dramatist who was a cripple as a writer, and this is lamentable but not ruinous'. Since then drama has tended increasingly to proceed from the premise that characters should not be

15

endowed with a greater fluency than their relatively inarticulate real-life counterparts. Logical enough, perhaps, and certainly it is 'not ruinous' if the dramatist is not a master of prose, let alone a poet. Yet in calling it 'lamentable', Miller implies that the general expectation of articulacy should not be set too low and that the drama ought not to be too quick to accept the role of a mere tape-recorder.

His own practice has usually been to lift the dialogue fractionally above the incoherencies of everyday intercourse while keeping it firmly grounded in the rhythm of ordinary speech and the idiom of the vernacular. His vocabulary is usually simple, but an idiosyncrasy of usage will give it freshness of meaning, as when Quentin, in *After the Fall,* exclaims 'How few the days are that hold the mind in place' or Victor, in *The Price,* tells his brother 'You can't walk in with one splash and wash out twenty-eight years'. It is not pretentious, it is not outside what one can imagine someone saying, but it does keep the audience listening and it insists quietly on the primacy of the spoken word in the theatre.

(4)

If this constitutes part of his attraction for the reader, it also explains in part the tendency to overstate the solemnity of his plays. It is sometimes implied that, like some of Shaw's, they are static in their preoccupation with polemical debate, ideas, and moral principles, but unalleviated by Shavian wit. In print they may give this impression but in the theatre, appropriately, their vitality is more immediately apparent. Harold Clurman, who has been involved in producing at least four of Miller's plays, describes him as 'a most meticulous craftsman' whose sense of theatre enables his texts to be realised on stage with the minimum of alteration or embellishments by the producer. Stagecraft and action are essential elements of his drama. The inventiveness with which he has liberated himself from the constrictions of the proscenium arch is as remarkable as the skill with which, when it has suited his purpose, he has worked imaginatively within its confines. The phrase beloved of the film-promoters, 'action-packed drama', could hardly be applied even to *A View from the Bridge,* yet the tense atmosphere generated in that play culminates in two or three moments of physical violence managed and timed with such dexterity that many theatre-goers will recall these as dominating the entire production. The reversal in the closing minutes of *The Crucible* when John Proctor confesses and then recants his confession may, in the describing, sound like an old and over-worked dramatic device, but in the theatre it makes a quite different impact. The alternation, in *Death of a Salesman*, between past and present, shadow and substance, can also be made to sound like a cliché, but that is not how it comes across on the stage.

(5)

Yet Miller's plays are in important ways intensely personal. In a letter in 1949 he commented :

> However, it is obvious that I write out of life as I know it, rather than construct plays out of a theatrical imagination, as it were. The remembered thing about *Salesman* is really the basic situation in which these people find themselves, a situation which I have seen repeated throughout my life.[5]

That we remember other things about the play as well does not detract from the accuracy and feeling with which the basic situation is observed and dramatised. His remark on another occasion that all his plays are in a sense autobiographical will come as no surprise to any sensitive reader, but it ought not to encourage the scholar into arid grubbing after the sources of incidents in plays or the original on which this and that character is based.

Not easy to define but certainly crucial to his work is the fact of his Jewishness. Mary McCarthy detected the rhythms of Jewish speech in *Death of a Salesman* and another critic finds evidence of a 'de-Semitising process' at work in the early plays, but it is really only after 1960 that the Jewish element becomes important in his drama.[6] In his prose fiction it features earlier but in characteristically controlled form. Thus the perceptive novel *Focus* (1945) treats anti-Semitism by exploring the dilemma of a Gentile mistaken for a Jew: and when he first wished to present on the stage similar problems of ethnicity and alienation it is typical of his tact and intelligence that he did so in the context, not of a Jewish ghetto, but of a Sicilian immigrant community of Brooklyn longshoremen. It is also a truism, but one that has to be re-stated, that his strong faith in the solidarity of the family, and particularly his uneasiness at any threat to or

17

failure in the role of the father, are largely attributable to his ethnic origins. The Jewish experience in the Second World War became an explicit theme in his plays first in *After the Fall* and *Incident at Vichy*. More recently he has explored it with great depth of feeling in the television film *Playing for Time*.

Growing up in the Depression has also affected Miller in ways more subtle and complex than one would infer from the nostalgia of his autobiographical essay 'A Boy grew in Brooklyn'[7] or even the more bitter-sweet *Memory of Two Mondays*. 'It was a good time to be growing up', he has said, 'because nobody else knew anything either'; but he also comments 'Nobody could escape that disaster', and it is this image of the Depression that predominates in his plays, especially in *The American Clock*. The earlier plays bear traces of attitudes inherited from the 1930s and of the association with the Federal Theater Project that taught him his craft. His political awareness too was moulded in those days, but it was sharpened in the 1950s by the McCarthyite anti-Communist witch hunts with which he dealt obliquely in *The Crucible*.

His own appearance, in 1956, before the House Un-American Activities Committee focused poignantly for him the problems of moral choice on which his plays so often turn. He chose not to incriminate people he knew, and his conviction in 1957 for contempt of Congress (even though no punishment was imposed and the conviction was reversed the following year by the Supreme Court) must have intensified that sense of the vulnerability of the social non-conformist that he had dramatised so effectively in 1950 in his adaptation of Ibsen's *An Enemy of the People*.

The quiet dignity with which Miller refused to name names earned him much respect in the press. *The New Republic* described him as 'the passionately self-exploring, artist-genius type'. Less crudely, it castigated the unscrupulous attack made on him by counsel at the hearing and continued :

> But Miller wouldn't fight back. He had never been under Communist discipline, he said, and he had explored — and rejected — the party's professed love for creative artists. Also he stayed cool and unemotional. We have never seen Miller before. He is impressive.

His plays have also been thought cool and unemotional

(sometimes too much so), but another event in his private life in 1956 implied anything but a lack of emotion. This was his marriage to Marilyn Monroe, the film actress who had just divorced the baseball player Joe DiMaggio. Miller had similarly just divorced his first wife after sixteen years of marriage; he and Marilyn Monroe were married in a civil ceremony and then remarried four days later in the Jewish faith. The marriage lasted for four years with an apparent stability that made the break-up more surprising even than its beginning.

Our concern will be only with the effect of the relationship on his creative work and whether, as is sometimes charged, he exploited his personal experiences in too nakedly exhibitionist a manner in his plays after his third marriage (to the Austrian-born photographer Inge Morath) in 1962. These experiences, public and private, indisputably intensified for him the moral sense of guilt and responsibility that has always formed the corner-stone of his plays; and, despite some aberrations, what the *New Republic* said of him as a witness may also be said of him as a dramatist : 'He is impressive'.

2

Three Early Plays

(1)

As an undergraduate at the University of Michigan Miller achieved, with at least two plays, a success that did not attend his first Broadway piece, *The Man Who Had All the Luck* (1944). It won a Theatre Guild prize, and the shortness of its run attracted from the *Burns Mantle Yearbook* the comment that this 'unusually interesting and well-played comedy was mistakenly withdrawn, it seemed to this writer, after only 4 performances. It was at least worth a three-week chance to find itself and its public'. Although Miller chose not to include it in *Collected Plays,* its anticipations of the later works merit discussion.

In the printed version (which is not identical with the version staged) David Frieber, a garage mechanic in a small mid-western country town, prospers in business and in private life by a series of chances, despite a conviction that things must sometime go wrong. Eventually, to satisfy himself that skill matters more than luck and the generosity of his friends that have so far shaped his life, he mortgages everything to start a mink-farm. Adverse weather conditions and a delivery of diseased fish threaten the success of the minks' whelping, on which everything is staked, but disaster might still have been averted were it not that Hester, his wife, sensing his superstition, forces him to let them die : 'It's not that they must die. It's that you've got to kill them ... I want you to know once and for all that it was you who did it'. Like the characters in Miller's later plays, though more artificially, David is thus forced into an acceptance of moral responsibility.

The play's weaknesses are evident in the first act. The dramatisation of luck is always likely to strain coincidence but here the long arm quickly acquires proportions altogether too simian. Opposition to the orphan David's marriage is eliminated in the opening scene when Hester's father is killed

20

pushing the car on the repair of which David's career is to be based. His technical skill is inadequate to detect and repair the fault in the time given, but it is done for him while he sleeps. We may accept the nocturnal ministrations of fairy-folk in a tale by Grimm, but it is another thing to believe that a newly-arrived garage-proprietor would choose the middle of the night for his first call on a rival and would then be so accommodating as to save the situation for him.

Moreover, the stage is cluttered with a superfluity of minor characters who seem to have moved in from Winesburg, Ohio, and lost something in the process. The crippled store-keeper and David's fuddled aunt serve no real dramatic purpose. The car-owner need not make an appearance at all, and it is prodigal as well as unnecessary to bring Hester's father on the stage for two minutes in order to run him over in the wings as soon as he leaves. It is theatrical tact that is lacking here, and self-confidence. Miller tries to create the sense of a community, a real town, by crowding the stage with people in a spirit of mistaken naturalism. There is no real reason why the opening scene should be a store, but the stage-directions are meticulous in their cataloguing of the hardware on display and of the furnishings. In the second scene the car is actually on stage, its engine is started and the repairs are begun in full view of the audience.

At the play's climax, when Hester urges David to let the mink die, sentimental sententiousness takes over. 'Davey, you're a good man, good with your hands' equates virtue with dexterity far more portentously than does Linda Loman's praise for the do-it-yourself skill of her salesman husband, who was also 'good with his hands'. David talks like a character from *The Grapes of Wrath* :

> I stood in the world with money in my hands and everything was 'mine'! It was not *mine,* nothing is mine but what I'm good enough to make. Money is a bitch, Hester, it's a whore bitch that'll bear for any man and what it bears can never really be yours. Only these animals are mine. In the whole world they're the only things that would have died if I weren't there to make them live!

The emotionalised stage-direction is similarly Steinbeckian : 'He turns slowly away toward the open door as though feeling the dying of his mink. She steps away from him as though from a child first learning to stand'.

Well-meant indignation and intensity of moral earnestness provide the motivation even in minor aspects. Thus the store-keeper is a war-veteran who has lost his legs and who has been soured both by his disablement and by the irony that it was sustained, not on the battlefield, but after the Armistice when a boiler exploded in a Paris brothel; he has no real relevance to the story and seems to belong with *A Farewell to Arms* rather than to the nineteen-forties. His reiterated opinion that 'A man is a jelly-fish washed up on the beach' is repudiated by the play's moral; it is never adequately explored or developed.

(2)

Miller remarks that 'far from being a waste and failure this play was a preparation and possibly a necessary one, for those that followed'. This he connects, somewhat cryptically, with his sudden recognition that 'two of the characters ... were logically brothers and had the same father'. When the play was staged the hero's surname was accordingly changed to Beeves. A sub-plot had already been concerned with Patterson Beeves and his son Amos. Bringing David into the family deprives him of the orphan status that had heightened the fairy-tale quality of the earlier version, but it establishes a dramatic pattern central to much of Miller's work.

Patterson Beeves has devoted his life and energy to the dream of turning Amos into a champion baseball player, only to see him rejected by a talent scout in one of the play's most moving scenes. To Patterson's uncomprehending explanation of the intensive winter indoor training he has devised for the boy, the scout replies : 'Yeah, that's just where you made your mistake, Mr. Beeves'; and when Patterson tells him Amos 'doesn't know how to do anything else', his reply is the same : 'I guess that was another mistake'. By making David Amos's brother, Miller gives Patterson one son whom he destroys through a misplaced desire for his success, and another who survives the parental devotion, though he is not unscathed by it. It is the story of the Kellers in *All My Sons* and the Lomans in *Death of a Salesman*. The parallel to the latter is accentuated by the use of the folklore dream of success through prowess on the games-field and by the identical terms of abuse ('fake' and 'liar') that both Amos Patterson and Biff Loman apply to their fathers, although Willy's betrayal of Biff is far more complex and more far-reaching morally than Patterson's of Amos.

Whether, in the stage version, David's brother relationship to Amos was emphasised by any other changes, I do not know, but Miller seems to have perceived the theme's full implications only gradually in the first three plays in which it occurs. Of the 'destroyed' sons, Amos is passive, dumb and dramatically uninteresting. Larry Keller is dead before the play opens, but his recognition of his father's guilt, conveyed in his letter to his fiancée, is more articulate and more morally perceptive than Amos's. Biff is the most 'aware' of the three, the most fully portrayed, and the one whose betrayal disturbs us most.

To the other brother Miller's attitude changes more sharply. David is the play's central figure and the man who had all the luck. Chris Keller is prompted by a stronger moral indignation and is faced with bigger problems : he has learnt in the war that he can fail, but he has also learnt to live with that knowledge and to build on it. He still has a lot of the luck, and he retains something of David's superstitious guilt, though its motivation is made more acceptable by his description to his fiancée, Ann, of the death of his company of soldiers. His idealistic social conscience makes him the object of an envy and a resentment more true-to-life than the benevolence David's luck inspired in his friends. Ann's brother embodies it particularly, but a neighbour has already put it more caustically ('I resent living next door to the Holy Family'), and even Ann warns Chris of his tendency to idealise his friends. In the earlier play David's effect on people is described by his benefactor J.B. Feller : 'Everytime I set eyes on him something happens to me. I suddenly feel that everything is possible again'. In *All My Sons* this effect becomes more ambivalent.

> SUE (*With growing feeling*): Chris makes people want to be better than it's possible to be. He does that to people ... My husband has a family, dear. Everytime he has a session with Chris he feels as though he's compromising by not giving up everything for research. As though Chris or anybody else isn't compromising. [pp.130-131][8]

J.B. Feller and Jim Bayliss, Sue's husband, stand in the same relationship to the younger heroes of the two plays and represent the same values of good-neighbourliness. The difference between them is not merely that an external critic of

Jim is provided for us in Sue: in *All My Sons* the claims of family responsibility have become much more complex, and idealism is judged not *per se* but in terms of the conflicts it provokes.

Chris is the most attractive, the most decent, of the three versions of that character. David is wooden by comparison and less human but, like him, Chris learns a responsible independence. After his confession of guilt it is again the woman who tells him, almost in the words Hester had used : 'Because you mustn't feel that way any more. Because you have a right to whatever you have. Everything, Chris, understand that? To me, too ... And the money, there's nothing wrong in your money'[p.122]. In saying that, Ann knows something of his father's guilt but is realistic enough to recognise that Chris bears no part of it. The change that the Chris-character undergoes, however, before his re-incarnation in the next play is striking.

'Happy' Loman has lost all the conscientious scruples of David and Chris to become as demoralised as his brother but in a more cynical way. Happy accepts his father's standards without fighting them, and has the adaptability necessary to make them work for himself. He no longer needs any of the luck: he is the smooth operator who gets what he wants by having the personality to take it. It emerges in his conversation with Biff :

> That girl Charlotte I was with tonight is engaged to be married in five weeks ... The guy's in line for the vice-presidency of the store. I don't know what gets into me, maybe I just have an overdeveloped sense of competition or something, but I went and ruined her, and furthermore I can't get rid of her. And he's the third executive I've done that to. Isn't that a crummy characteristic? And to top it all, I go to their weddings![p.19]

Of David another character has said that he 'is not comfortable unless everybody he knows is as happy as himself. He suffers sometimes from an over-developed sense of responsibility'. The change, in what is basically the same character, from 'an over-developed sense of responsibility' to 'an overdeveloped sense of competition or something' is a convenient index to the shift from inner-direction to other-direction that David Riesman and his collaborators were charting sociologically at about the time that Miller was writing

Death of a Salesman[9]. It also reflects Miller's maturing disillusion in this David/Chris/Happy character, and even more, his growing awareness of the importance of the father-character.

After *Death of a Salesman* the focus shifts back to the brothers. Quentin and Dan, in *After the Fall,* are contrasted in their attitudes to the father ruined in the Depression. On this identical contrast *The Price* is based, and here the theme receives its fullest treatment : for the first time the father is not seen on stage at all but remains a strongly-felt presence throughout. Even in *The Creation of the World, and Other Business* the Cain and Abel element explores a similar fraternal antagonism. All these will be discussed in their turn, but *The Man Who Had All the Luck* has other links with *All My Sons*.

(3)

Both originated in real-life anecdotes that Miller had heard, both have a mid-western setting and atmosphere, both are cast in the same dramatic mould. The fussily realistic detail of the set recurs in *All My Sons* but this time it is concentrated into one location throughout and an element of symbolism is introduced by the use of the tree. The cast-list is smaller than its predecessor by only one, and although the characters are, on the whole, more skilfully utilised, more fully developed, and more dramatically relevant, it is arguable that the sense of a neighbourhood community could have been more economically evoked. The small boy Bert is readily dispensable, and the Lubeys contribute little to the essential action.

Nevertheless, the advance on *The Man Who Had All the Luck* is evident both in theme and technique. An aircraft-engine manufacturer with no conscience who supplies faulty cylinder-heads in wartime is likely to command more attention and to raise wider issues than a mink-farming mechanic with a conscience at once too sensitive and too narrow. However, it is primarily at the domestic level that the problem is explored; the real value of the war framework lies in its topicality, in the audience-indignation that is universally generated against Joe Keller, and in the social tension and guilt set up in his sons. But there is never any question of these emotions prompting Chris to any form of political action or public protest — a point too

25

obvious to need making, except that references to the play too often suggest that it is politically-directed.

Miller's achievement here, to put it at its lowest, lies in the verisimilitude with which he creates not only a convincing homely family, but also the sense of the flow of communal life in a suburban neighbourhood. The Kellers are part of a town in a way that the Beeves never were. Indeed, the atmosphere of American neighbourliness is allowed to become so predominant that we are not kept sufficiently aware of the latent hostility to Joe that is mentioned from time to time.

Joe himself is too pleasant for the part he has to play. His betrayal of his partner seems out of key with his simple geniality and warmth of nature. As with most of Miller's characters, there is no vice in him, only littleness and his own form of myopia. He is genuinely unable to visualise the public consequences of what was for him a private act. To have stopped production when the flaw was discovered would have endangered the future of the business that meant security for his family: it was as simple as that. Keller is no villainous capitalist egged on by competitive mania in a cut-throat world of business, nor is he the cynical profiteer deliberately reducing the margin of safety in order to increase the margin of profit. Miller sees him as the simple man who has got on by energy and will power but who is hardly clever enough to know how he has done it. To this extent he is another man who has had 'all the luck' and there is more than a grain of truth in his wife's comment to their son: 'We're dumb, Chris. Dad and I are stupid people. We don't know anything. You've got to protect us' [p.127]. He is the ordinary man, surprised that 'every week a new book comes out' [p.96], occasionally uncertain of his pronunciation, aggressively proud of his night-school education, yet moved to embarrassed facetiousness by his son's knowledge of French, and perplexed by a world where 'you stand on the street today and spit, you're gonna hit a college man' [p.134]. Yet even these traits are only sporadically evident: it is the man's *bonhomie,* sense of fun, and good nature that predominate. If we come to accept the idea of this man deliberately allowing his partner to take the blame for shipping the faulty engines and thinking to patch up his conscience as easily as the flaws were patched to delay detection — and we do accept it in the theatre — it is primarily because of the dramatic

26

effectiveness with which the climax and *dénouement* are brought about. Only later do we realise that it is in character, that it is the reverse of the coin of which the obverse has seemed so attractive, and that the coin is of smaller demonination than we thought, but none the less still a recognisable part of the currency.

The improvement in dramatic effectiveness may be immediately illustrated from the act-endings. In *The Man Who Had All the Luck* the direction 'Slow Curtain' repeated at the end of most of its five scenes recalls too readily Miller the student-dramatist who had had to ask a friend how long an act ought to be. There is not the climactic use of the curtain that is achieved naturally in *All My Sons* even in the first, relatively slow-moving act. The second act is brought to an explosive but perfectly-timed conclusion, and the superbly-developed tension of the play's ending is blurred only by the bringing of Chris back on to the stage for his mother's final and uncharacteristically wise comment. The impulse to prolong the action of *Death of a Salesman* beyond the death of its protagonist is more defensible than this, if only because the central issue of *All My Sons* is simpler and the suicide of Joe Keller dramatically more self-justifying, for the events leading up to it have been presented with a directness and an increasing tempo that make any alternative impossible. By contrast to Miller's skilful observance of the old unities in *All My Sons* the episodic structure of *The Man Who Had All the Luck,* with its dramatic confusion, loss of pace, and irrelevancies of character and action, seems almost amateurish.

The objection is sometimes made that *All My Sons* is so well-constructed as to be unconvincing, and the delayed revelation of Ann's third-act production of the letter from Larry is instanced as meretricious playmanship. On the other hand, her reluctance to produce it earlier is credibly enough explained by her, and it would not be easy to devise a more economical — or a more telling — method of bringing home the two things essential to the action at that point : the demolition of the mother's dream that her son is still alive and the demonstration to Joe, in terms that he cannot escape, of the consequences of his own conduct. Whether Ann, with that knowledge, would have been quite so sympathetic to Joe earlier in the play is another question, but one that Joe's irresistible

27

geniality and Ann's nostalgia for the past go part of the way to answering, especially as she has earlier accepted the court's verdict that the blame was her own father's rather than Joe's.

The confident certainty of dramatic movement here seems deliberately and successfully counterpoised against the loss of certainty that is the play's main theme. The keynote of the play is its questioning. Dialogue in the theatre is regularly carried on in terms of questions and answers, but in *All My Sons* the questions are in effect dialogue-stoppers. The dramatic power resides in the sort of questions asked and in the inability of the characters to answer them. Particularly prominent in the last act and in the exchanges between Joe and his son, this is observable throughout, and is responsible for the powerful climax to the second act in Chris's agonised reiteration of such questions as 'Where do you live, where have you come from?... What must I do, Jesus God, what must I do?' Nothing brings out Joe Keller's bewildered isolation better than this exchange with his wife :

KELLER: Maybe I ought to talk to [Ann]?

MOTHER: Don't ask me, Joe.

KELLER *(almost an outburst)*: Then who do I ask? But I don't think she'll do anything about it.

MOTHER: You're askin' me again.

KELLER: I'm askin' you. What am I, a stranger? I thought I had a family here. What happened to my family?

MOTHER: You've got a family. I'm simply telling you that I have no strength to think any more ....

KELLER: Then what do I do? Tell me, talk to me, what do I do? [pp.161-162]

A few minutes later, among questions to his son, he interjects the same plea : 'Talk to me'.

This is the bewilderment of a naturally garrulous man who has suddenly realised the impossibility of communication on the matters of deepest consequence, and it is a dilemma which the often-criticised banality of Miller's dramatic idiom is particularly well suited to suggest. Against these baffled questions and the clichés of his quotidian conversation Joe's final statement in the play stands out with an integrity and a force far in excess of its verbal content. His decision is made and his question answered by the letter of his dead son :

MOTHER: You're so foolish. Larry was your son too, wasn't he? You know he'd never tell you to do this.

KELLER: *(looking at letter in his hand)*: Then what is this if it isn't telling me? Sure, he was my son. But I think to him they were all my sons. And I guess they were, I guess they were. [p.170]

That is almost the only statement in this play of questioning that should be taken at its face value, and its quiet dignity makes Chris's summing-up ('there's a universe of people outside and you're responsible to it') superfluous and gratuitously didactic. The other and more sensational statements must be seen in their immediate context. 'This is the land of the great big dogs, you don't love a man here, you eat him! That's the principle'[p.167] — it is not Miller who says this, but Chris, and Chris the baffled idealist *in extremis*. Its hysterical note distinguishes it from the more responsible tone of genuine recognition in Joe's speech. The play is a social drama, not as an attack on the capitalist business ethic, but as a study of the bewildered common man groping in a world where moral values have become a shifting quicksand, where you ask for guidance from others no surer than yourself, and when the simplest lesson — moral responsibility to others — is the hardest to learn.

(4)

It has become a commonplace of criticism to link this play with Ibsen and to see it as another version of, for example, *Pillars of Society*. Miller's attitude to Ibsen, however, may be better illustrated by ignoring chronology for the moment, and turning to his adaptation of *An Enemy of the People,* which was staged in 1950. He undertook this

working from a pidgin-English word-for-word rendering of the Norwegian... because I had a private wish to demonstrate that Ibsen is really pertinent today, that he is not 'old-fashioned' and, implicitly, that those who condemn him are themselves misleading our theatre and our playwrights into a blind alley of senseless sensibility, triviality, and the inevitable waste of our dramatic talents.[10]

Miller makes changes in three areas : language, structure, and ideas. The first is the most obvious and the least important from our present point of view. Not only purists will have their doubts about 'Well, what do you say to a little hypodermic for these fence-sitting deadheads?' as an alternative to the more usual versions (e.g. 'Don't you think it is high time we stirred a little life into all this slackness and vacillation and cowardice?')[11]. But this is an extreme instance, and more usually Miller's dialogue is racy and modern without being as aggressively colloquial as this.

He turns it into a three-act play with two scenes in each of the first two acts (corresponding to Ibsen's first four acts) and one in the last (Ibsen's fifth), but for the reader's convenience I have adhered, in my references, to Ibsen's divisions. More important structural changes are mainly in the nature of abridgements of some passages of dialogue : Miller complains of 'Ibsen's insistence that his meaning be driven home — and from the front door right through to the back, lest the audience fail to understand him'. Thus the interviews between Hovstad and Stockmann in Act II, and between Hovstad, Aslaksen, and Billing in Act III, are shortened, the pace of Act V is accelerated, and Act IV (the public meeting) is modified in several respects. The scene opens differently and less use is generally made of the crowd. Peter Stockmann wrecks his brother's presentation of his case expertly and economically without the help of Hovstad and Billing that Ibsen gives him; and Stockmann's belief in the evolution of a natural aristocracy of leaders disappears entirely.

Miller's preface attributes this last omission to his desire to avoid fascist or *Herrenvolk* implications that he feels Ibsen did not intend. This is over-cautious and helps to support one adverse criticism of the adaptation as

a perversion of the original in that it transformed the hero into a conventional modern liberal and thus rested the case for him rather upon the supposed correctness of his ideas than upon the abstract right of dissent even if it be a dissent from what passes among the intellectuals for right thinking.[12]

For a writer with Miller's liberal outlook this is perhaps inevitable, and some of his other departures from the original have a similar effect. Thus Billing's statement in Act I, 'A community is like a ship; everyone ought to be prepared to take the helm', is 'democratised' by Miller into 'every man should do something to help navigate the ship.' Stockmann's hope is that the wealth from the springs will help his compatriots to become 'more like Men, more like A People'; and the scene in Act III, where Stockmann in boisterous high spirits assumes the Mayor's hat and stick and is then obliged to surrender them, is in Miller's version embellished with the following didactic pomposity :

> I just wanted you to realize, Peter *(he takes off the hat and looks at it)* that anyone may wear this hat in a democracy, and that a free citizen is not afraid to touch it. *(He hands him the hat.)* And as for the baton of command, Your Honor, it can pass from hand to hand. *(He hands the cane to* Peter Stockmann.) So don't gloat yet. The people haven't spoken. [p.79]

If the collocation of these quotations out of their contexts suggests a campaign-address, other speeches in the play remind us that at the back of such sentiments there lies a long tradition of American literary, as well as party-political, thought. When Stockmann's sons return from school at the end of the second scene, Miller makes them tell their father they have learnt at school what an insect is. He replies : 'You know what I'm going to do, boys? From now on I'm going to teach you what a man is'. The theme of his lessons, presumably, will be Emersonian : 'Whoso would be a man must be a nonconformist'; and by implication at least 'the abstract right of dissent' is supported, as it is again later when Stockmann insists on the need for the pioneer : 'Before many can know something, *one* must know it'. Similarly, one of Miller's additions to Ibsen is also Emersonian in sentiment if not entirely in expression : 'Oh God, on the wreckage of all the civilizations in the world there ought to be a big sign : "They Didn't Dare!".' The case for conformity is put by the Mayor in conventional terms and anticipates one issue that underlies *The Crucible* :

> You have an ingrained tendency to go your own way, Thomas, and that simply can't go on in a well-organised society. The individual really must subordinate himself to the over-all, or *(groping for words, he points to himself)* to the authorities who are in charge of the general welfare. [pp.26–27]

He can explain Thomas's nonconformity only in terms of vindictiveness and hatred of authority, adding a cliché that acquires on his lips an irony which one hopes Miller intends : 'This is the mad dream of a man who is trying to blow up our way of life'. [pp.74–75]

But, as in Ibsen, the last word is with Thomas Stockmann, and this receives a characteristic twist : what had earlier been rendered as 'The strongest man in the world is he who stands most alone' now appeared in this version (or inversion) :

> But remember now, everybody, you are fighting for the truth, and that's why you're alone. And that makes you strong. We're the strongest people in the world ... and the strong must learn to be lonely. [pp.124–125]

It is not only the possibly fortuitous overtones of counsel to the United States on the implications of international leadership that makes this so characteristically American, but the whole romanticisation of the loneliness of the high-principled individual. In the stage direction for Stockmann's last speech ('with a trembling mixture of trepidation and courageous insistence'), and in the speech itself, there is more than a hint of a sentimentalisation of loneliness.

Neighbourliness is a cardinal virtue in *All My Sons* and even in *An Enemy of the People* Miller's belief in the value of community comes through almost unexpectedly in Stockmann himself. In Ibsen's Act II the doctor had expressed his satisfaction at being able to do good in his own home town. Miller changes this to: 'You can't imagine the feeling, Catherine, to know that your own town feels like a brother to you. I have never felt so at home in this town since I was a boy'. By this emphasis on 'at-homeness' he brings the situation more closely into line with twentieth-century American values. Similarly, at the end of Act I, Stockmann's satisfaction at having done something for the community is transposed into a satisfaction at having 'earned the respect of one's neighbours'. This brings it uncomfortably close to Willy Loman's desire to be liked and even to be well liked.

Similarly, when Stockmann praises the moderate Aslaksen as 'a very sincere man' it is Willy and his contemporary society that come to mind. David Riesman had diagnosed the preoccupation with sincerity as meeting a psychological need rather than the political one that it purported to serve, and had remarked that 'Just because such a premium is put on sincerity,

32

Death of a Salesman: Lee J. Cobb (*Willy:* seated) in a scene from the Broadway production (New York 1949)

Death of a Salesman: Jo Mielziner's set (London, 1949)

Death of a Salesman:
Paul Muni (*Willy*),
(London, 1949)

Death of a Salesman:
Lee J. Cobb (*Willy*),
(New York, 1949)

a premium is put on faking it'. Miller seems to me to have come to this critical conclusion by his own route and to have embodied it better in Willy Loman than in his Americanisation of Stockmann two years later. Miller also seems to accept at its face value Stockmann's belief that the world can be remade by 'the strongest people' augmented by the dozen street urchins that Stockmann proposes to educate; the insistence that these boys should be 'good and ignorant, absolutely uncivilized' raises expectations of the arrival of Huckleberry Finn's raft.

Miller's debt to Ibsen, then, is not closely ideological, but what he learns from him dramatically may be seen from this adaptation. His streamlining of the play, so as to eliminate some of the ponderousness he complains of in Ibsen, has been already illustrated, but one minor improvement is made in the last scene by dovetailing Peter's exit with Kiil's entrance. In the original they were separated by three speeches, but their coinciding appears ironically to substantiate Peter's allegation of complicity between Stockmann and Kiil, and Peter's contemptuous snort as he leaves gives dramatic point to this.

Miller makes another, and less expected, change by increasing the element of humour. This is sometimes done by additions to the dialogue, such as Stockmann's warning to his brother in the last scene against sitting too close to the already-broken windows : 'Not there. A piece of the solid majority is liable to open your skull'. It is also effected by making the Mayor a little more comic in his pompous conservatism, but without playing down his more sinister characteristics. Rather more use is made of the drunken man at the meeting, and Billing's pseudo-liberalism also comes in for ridicule by being Americanised :

> Doctor Stockmann, I feel as though I were standing in some historic painting. Goddammit, this is a historic day! Someday this scene'll be in a museum, entitled 'The Day the Truth Was Born'! [p.66]

The main change, however, is in the role of Morten Kiil. A new opening to the play has Kiil finishing dinner at Stockmann's with Billing. He leaves as the Mayor arrives, but not before he has helped himself, unobserved, to apples and tobacco, and then, with polite shows of refusal, allowed his daughter to give him some more. His miserliness is throughout a source of comedy, and so is his inability to understand Stockmann's explanation of the nature of bacteria (this whole exchange is developed more amusingly and more fully than in Ibsen). Miller does not bring Kiil in to the public-meeting scene at all, which seems in character, and, without minimising his unscrupulousness in the last act, allows him to make his final exit on Aslaksen's arrival with the wry comment : 'Too many intellectuals here : I'd better go'. [p.115]

The humour that Miller injects, not unsuccessfully, into Ibsen's play has not been much in evidence in his own, at least until *The Price*. In these early plays such comic touches as there are seem intended simply to contribute to the realism of the whole. Although he jokes that Ibsen's plays 'have always been set forth with yards of fringe on every tablecloth and drapery', his version of *An Enemy of the People* cuts only a few inches off that fringe, and his own plays, before *Death of a Salesman,* belong, broadly speaking, in the same familiarly realistic convention.

(5)

The notices that *All My Sons* received were favourable in their tributes to his talent and theatrical craftsmanship, but, understandably, not out of the ordinary. Robert Garland in *Journal-American* is representative : 'It says something of moment about something of moment, it says it with controlled emotion and impressive skill. Frequently it is indignant, but always about the real and righteous things'.

That a sympathetic reviewer might have made the same comments on an early Ibsen play emphasises the perennial value of such drama. That the play should have been 'the play of the year' in 1949 suggests that the native American theatre and its critics were somewhat more conventionally-minded than the post-war European theatre. *All My Sons* is the least original, the least exploratory in theatrical technique, of all Miller's major plays; but, although it is interesting as a preparation for the later plays, it has enough vitality and importance to hold the stage on its own merits. I have seen its essential qualities brought out remarkably by an arena-stage production, with the minimum of properties, in a very small hall. The intimacy of this production certainly overcame any suggestion of the stiffness that the play is sometimes accused of, and brought out eloquently the human relationships on which the play is, like all

34

of Miller's, so firmly based. Shorn of its naturalistic setting, it gains rather than loses.

The problem with which Miller has always had to contend is how to keep in dramatic balance his natural ability to create human and sympathetic characters and his tendency to didactic moralisation of his scenes and themes. In the three plays discussed in this chapter the basic situation is credible enough but the didactic element is not tightly enough reined. The remaining plays all show more enterprise and originality in their experimentation with new means of achieving this balance, while at the same time, with the possible exception of *The Price,* they progressively widen the scope of his subjects. It is on them, rather than on these early works, that his reputation rests.

3

Death of a Salesman

The role of Willy Loman was created by Lee J. Cobb in Elia
Kazan's Broadway production of 1949. When the London
production opened five months later the part was played by
Paul Muni. This gratuitous piece of historical information
highlights conveniently a controversy about the play that still
persists and illustrates the stamp that an actor's interpretation
can leave on a drama. Looking back on the notices of these first
productions one could be forgiven for thinking that there were
two plays, the American *Death of a Salesman* and the British.

British reviewers, such as Harold Hobson, who had seen
both actors in the role emphasised the radical differences
between the two interpretations:

> Mr Cobb's Loman was a man rejoicing in his enormous vitality, and
> quite unaware of his essential uselessness, the realisation of which
> came upon him at the end as a shattering and incomprehensible
> paradox. Mr Muni's performance, on the other hand, was that of a
> sad little chap beaten from the start, pushed around by life and his
> fellows, pathetically incompetent, touching and exasperating by
> turns. Mr Cobb took the play along with splendid drive, but hardly
> ever unsealed the springs of pity. Mr Muni was frequently moving,
> but occasionally became a bore.[13]

In 1949 Hobson had been a little more sympathetic, observing
that 'on at least five occasions Mr Muni brings the entire
audience close to tears' and 'in the supreme moments of his
performance Mr Muni could not be surpassed'. To Philip Hope-
Wallace in New York the play had seemed 'something
comparable to an American *King Lear*' but comparison with
the London production made him 'regretfully withdraw' this:
unlike Cobb, Muni did not seem to feel that it was Willy's
'illusion (even as Lear's illusion of kingship) which made him
big by his own lights and makes his fall tragic'. Yet, as Audrey

Williamson was to point out, 'Willy's 'success' is a mirage that deceives no one but himself and Muni's crushed nervousness had a poignant reality'.[14]

Muni was already popular in England for stage and screen performances. *The Times* captioned its photograph of the play 'Mr. Muni's Return' and several reviews approached it primarily as a vehicle for him. For J.C. Trewin, indeed, Muni was the play's only redeeming feature : his review read, in its entirety :

> *Death of a Salesman*, Arthur Miller's American play at the Phoenix, was almost the death of a critic. Happily, Paul Muni is in the cast to play the little salesman with a pathetic belief in his worthless son, and his vigour and humanity help to relieve an evening that is otherwise tangled, pretentious, and dull. It is, however, a commercial success.[15]

This is out of key with most other British reviews only in its hostility in the play : Trewin's emphasis on 'the little salesman' as a pathetic figure was echoed by many others. The British *Death of a Salesman* established itself as a moving story of human failure, the self-destruction of a little man; the American is an examination of the impact on an ordinary, though not necessarily little, salesman of a national success-ethic. 'The American Dream' was a phrase less current in Britain in the 1940s than it has since become. It envisages a society in which success through his own efforts is still as available to the ordinary man as it was in the expansive, pioneering days of the last century; looking back nostalgically to the simpler, homely values of those days, it also looks forward to the possibility of grasping opportunity with equal vigour in modern circumstances so that sturdy, independent enterprise will be rewarded by a sense of achievement, improved living conditions for the individual and his family, and, in all probability, affluence. An audience nourished on such beliefs would naturally be alert to evidence of them in Willy's aspirations and would be sympathetic to his dismay at a changing world in which they seem no longer capable of realisation. Only one or two British reviewers, however, saw Willy as essentially American, though to a number he was, in the words of *Theatre World*, ' "Everyman" once again, in our day and generation, more blind than ever to the real spiritual values of life'. Of those thus disposed to see it as a morality play none (perhaps surprisingly) thought of it as a Marxist or even a left-wing morality, yet in New York, of course, those tags were much more readily applied.

Differing national attitudes towards communism at that time might explain this. The name of Elia Kazan was less well-known here than it is now, and less well-known than in America; both he and Lee J. Cobb had been in the original cast of the 1935 Group Theater production of Clifford Odets's *Waiting for Lefty*, a circumstance which, coupled with Miller's connection with the Federal Theater Project, may have predisposed some Americans to expect a play more redolent of the thirties than would an English audience. Audrey Williamson was to recall that Kazan and Cobb had both been in the 1938 London production of Odets's *Golden Boy ;* she had evidently been much impressed by that play and by the work of the Group Theater, but no London reviewer in 1949 made this connection. The Muni reading could have lent itself to the anti-capitalist emphasis so often put on the play, but it does not seem to have done so : Hobson's 'sad little chap' is 'pushed around by life and his fellows', not by forces more sinister.

One critic's description of it as 'a deeply understanding study of a once happy family torn to pieces by forces outside its comprehension'[16] is typical. *The Times* felt that 'this massive and relentless play' falls into two halves, of which the first shows 'the straits in which an unnatural civilisation places natural man', and 'the second, and much better, half of the play' concentrates on the father/son relationship with a sense of the tragic which 'amply makes up for the overwhelming accumulation of detail with which the dramatist prepares for it'. The word to which most British reviewers sooner or later had recourse was 'moving', but they were moved emotionally, not politically.

(2)

Its 742 New York performances immediately put it into the *Burns Mantle Yearbook* list of the fifty longest recorded Broadway runs (including musicals) and it remained in that list until 1960. Such success did not prevent — indeed, perhaps invited — hostility, and the question which has always bedevilled discussion of *Death of a Salesman* was quickly raised: is it a tragedy? Eric Bentley, abroad when it opened in February 1949, attacked it on his return, hitting hard at everything from the lighting to the language, but especially at what he saw as the play's conflicting aims :

> The 'tragedy' destroys the social drama; the social drama keeps the 'tragedy' from having a genuinely tragic stature. By this last remark I mean that the theme of this social drama, as of most others, is *the little man as victim*. The theme arouses pity but no terror. Man is here too little and too passive to play the tragic hero.
>
> More important even than this, the tragedy and the social drama actually conflict. The tragic catharsis reconciles us to, or persuades us to disregard, precisely those material conditions which the social drama calls our attention to ... Or is Mr Miller a 'tragic' artist who without knowing it has been confused by Marxism?[17]

Exactly the reverse hypothesis was advanced by Eleanor Clark in *Partisan Review;* she saw Miller as a Marxist who had been confused by tragedy :

> It is, of course, the capitalist system that has done Willy in; the scene in which he is brutally fired after some forty years with the firm comes straight from the party-line literature of the thirties, and the idea emerges lucidly enough through all the confused motivations of the play that it is our particular form of money economy that has bred the absurdly false ideals of both father and sons. It emerges, however, like a succession of shots from a duck-blind. Immediately after every crack the playwright withdraws behind an air of pseudo-universality, and hurries to present some cruelty or misfortune due either to Willy's own weakness, as when he refuses his friend's offer of a job after he has been fired, or gratuitously from some other source, as in the quite unbelievable scene of the two sons walking out on their father in the restaurant.

The whole play, for Miss Clark, is characterised by 'an intellectual muddle and a lack of candor that regardless of Mr. Miller's conscious intent are the main earmark of contemporary fellow-travelling. What used to be a roar has become a whine'.

At about the time of the play's opening, Miller himself, interviewed by *New York Times,* stressed the tragic intention :

> The tragic feeling is evoked in us when we are in the presence of a character who is ready to lay down his life, if need be, to secure one thing — his sense of personal dignity.

Important as this idea is in Miller's later plays, it was confusing when associated with *Death of a Salesman,* for critics were quick to point out what the play itself demonstrated — that Willy Loman's sense of personal dignity was too precariously based to give him heroic stature. Since then it has become tediously conventional for the writers of books surveying modern drama to praise the play's social realism but hurriedly to add that, of course, it falls short of tragedy and is therefore disqualified as a 'great play'. (This complaint is usually associated with strictures on its unpoetic use of language.)

What is irritating about such criticism is its assured conviction that the mixture of social drama and tragedy is unintentional, and its implication, that, if Miller had only been clear-minded enough to concentrate on one or the other, a better play would have resulted. Eric Bentley is perfectly right to see it as a play about 'the little man as victim', but less right when he seems to prefer the little man to be a victim of only one thing, and to assume that a 'social drama' must be a socialist drama. The Marxist plays of Clifford Odets had rarely communicated a sense of the complex density of the society they criticised, and merely to show the little man as the victim of capitalist big business would, in 1949, have been to repeat what Elmer Rice had done in *The Adding Machine* twenty-six years earlier.

The evidence for a Marxist interpretation of *Death of a Salesman* is not very impressive. The scene in which Willy, seeking a change of job, is unceremoniously dismissed can hardly have been intended as the indictment of capitalism that Miss Clark thinks it. Theatrically it is a moving, even painful, scene, but it engenders a mixture of pity and exasperation rather than the indignation that we would expect of 'party-line literature'. Willy's behaviour is not calculated to enhance his or our sense of his personal dignity; even as we pity him for his despairing reduction of the wage he will settle for, we are exasperated by his inability to see that, by his obtuse mishandling of Howard, he is throwing away any chance he may have. The central irony of this scene resides in the discrepancy between Howard and our preconceived idea of the capitalist tycoon. This is no ruthless executive callously firing the trusted employee from calculated mercenary motives : it is the 'nice guy' forced into a situation that he doesn't know how to handle 'nicely' and consequently only making the ugliness of it worse.

40

It is one little man being fired by another little man, Willy being fired by a younger Willy.

Howard's callousness is occasioned less by his business acumen than by his absorption in his personal life. The tape-recorder serves two purposes in the scene : when Willy stumbles against it and sets it accidentally into motion it precipitates an hysterical breakdown that symbolises the central theme of the play in Willy's horror at his inability to switch it off — to switch off the recorded past. Whether the past is that of his own sons recorded on his memory and conscience, or that of Howard's son recorded on a mechanical instrument, it is the past, more than capitalism, of which Willy is always the victim. The machine also provides a means of dramatising Howard's ingenuous pride in his children. They are far more real to him than is the memory of his father to which Willy constantly appeals, and his pride in their prowess and in their affection for him obliterates any understanding of Willy's plight, exactly as Willy's pride in his sons has blinded him to any recognition of the worth of Bernard. This point is emphasised by Howard's automatic question, 'Why don't your sons give you a hand?' and by the immediate introduction of the Ben-*motif* as a further reproach to Willy's vacillatory sentimentality.

Moreover, this memory-sequence dissolves into the actuality of Charley's office, where a successful Bernard on his way to professional and social triumphs in Washington unintentionally prompts Willy into another orgy of envious recrimination at everybody except himself. The irony set in motion in Howard's office culminates in Charley's, for it is Charley, not Howard, who is the nearest thing to the big business-man in this play, and yet Charley is the only person who offers Willy any positive help. The money he advances him and the employment he offers have no strings attached : Willy's acceptance of the one and rejection of the other is the outcome of a very curious sense of personal dignity, but there is no mistaking the truth of his exit line : 'Charley, you're the only friend I got. Isn't that a remarkable thing?'

It is remarkable to Willy not only because he has never had any time for Charley, but because Charley is the exact antithesis of himself. To describe Charley as the Horatio to Willy's Hamlet (as at least one critic has done) is to put it too romantically, but the antithesis is clearly and succinctly drawn

41

by Willy's exchange with Charley over Bernard's success :

WILLY: And you never told him what to do, did you? You never took any interest in him.

CHARLEY: My salvation is that I never took any interest in anything. There's some money — fifty dollars. I got an accountant inside. [p.75]

Charley the successful business-man is the only person who understands Willy the failed salesman, but he understands him in a wholly unsentimental way quite different from the 'interest' that is Willy's more characteristic response. He will help Willy with a job or with money, but he will not tell him what to do; he expects Willy, like Bernard, to make his own choice. Having subordinated sentiment to business efficiency all his life, Charley can allow his feelings to come through at Willy's funeral, and his final speech, 'Nobody dast blame this man . . . ,' though it is not the moral of the play, ought to have made unnecessary Miller's prefatory disavowal of any intended arraignment of big business.

This tacit acceptance of business as long as it is kept distinct from sentiment is not a noticeably Marxist position. Yet Miller does not seem to intend a criticism of Howard for dismissing Willy ('when a man gets old you fire him, you have to, he can't do the work') : but he contrives that dismissal so as to show Howard in as un-business-like a light as possible. The way in which Lawrence Newman is fired in Miller's novel *Focus,* on far more slender grounds, makes a marked contrast to this scene. Newman is being efficiently sacrificed to business efficiency where Willy, himself a bungler, is being dismissed by a man no better than himself. To this extent we sympathise with Willy's dilemma, but our respect is not given to either party, and the dramatic impact of this scene, properly played, ought to be one of inevitability — neither has any real alternative — and of littleness — neither is himself big enough to see the other, or to transcend his own sentimentality.

Even Willy's eulogy of old Dave Singleman, who 'was eighty-four years old, and he'd drummed merchandise in thirty-one states' and who 'died the death of a salesman', has to be seen, for all its subdued eloquence, in this light. Strategically placed in this key scene, it constitutes a criticism of Willy in its garrulous irrelevance to his situation, and at the same time it is a

42

condemnation of Howard for his failure to grasp its significance for Willy. Yet how little even this myth really means to Willy is ironically underlined in the next scene, when, tempted by Ben's offer of Alaskan wealth, he needs to be reminded of it by Linda:

> BEN: What are you building? Lay your hand on it. Where is it?
> WILLY *(hesitantly)*: That's true, Linda, there's nothing.
> LINDA: Why? *(To Ben:)* There's a man eighty-four years old.....
> WILLY: That's right, Ben, that's right. When I look at that man I say, what is there to worry about?[p.67]

Ben's contemptuous 'Bah!' is well-merited by the aura that this has of a piece of family folk-lore, a germ of Willy's self-deception to which Linda has been so repeatedly exposed that she has caught the infection worse than he has.

Conflicting with the salesman-ideal of success in a capitalist-commercial society, there is the pioneer-ideal of success in the 'great outdoors', represented for Willy not only in the person of Ben but in the idealised race-memory of the challenge of the frontier, embodied in his father, who drove a waggon-team right across the country selling flutes. There is also the popular image of success through sporting prowess : Biff the hero of the football field is another dream whereby Willy seeks his own identity. Neither of these is fully explored here; rather are they introduced as stereotypes to which the popular imagination always responds. Miller is very careful to insist on all these sets of ideals as *Willy's*. He deliberately provides no external documentation of Willy's memories of his own earlier success as a salesman. We hear of it only from Willy himself and, with less conviction, from Linda; Howard disputes it and Charley never offers any corroborative evidence. Similarly even the image of his waggon-driving father is something second-hand, not part of his own memory, but something he has been told of by Ben, who himself is not a character, but a creation of Willy's fancy. The title for the play was first to have been *The Inside of his Head,* a conception which deliberately precludes the external criteria required by tragedy. Tragedy also requires of its hero a final recognition of which, by his very nature, as well as by the nature of the play, Willy Loman is incapable.

Tragedy implies values; and to the repeated complaint that Willy has no values, Miller has replied in these terms :

The trouble with Willy Loman is that he has tremendously powerful ideals. We're not accustomed to speaking of ideals in his terms; but, if Willy Loman, for instance, had not had a very profound sense that his life as lived had left him hollow, he would have died contentedly polishing his car on some Sunday afternoon at a ripe old age. The fact is he has values. The fact that they cannot be realized is what is driving him mad — just as, unfortunately, it's driving a lot of other people mad. The truly valueless man, a man without ideals, is always perfectly at home anywhere.

Later in the same piece, however, Miller defined his aim in the play as being 'to set forth what happens when a man does not have a grip on the forces of life and has no sense of values which will lead him to that kind of a grip'.[18] The two statements are not, as some critics argue, contradictory. They are in fact reconciled by Biff's epitaph on his father : 'He had the wrong dreams. All, all wrong'. Charley's reply amounts to little more than a plea in mitigation : Willy *had* to dream. The only person who challenges Biff's verdict is Happy, who is by this stage of the play thoroughly discredited; and Willy's suicide itself implies some recognition, even though limited, of his wrong values.

Willy's inability to be 'always perfectly at home anywhere' proves in Miller's terms that he is not 'the truly valueless man'. Yet to be at home in the world is Willy's greatest desire; it is not an unworthy one, but it is certainly not the aspiration of a tragic hero.

(3)

In *Death of a Salesman* the difficulties in 'making of the outside world a home' are borne in on the spectator in the theatre by the set itself. In *All My Sons* the action takes place in 'the back yard of the Keller home . . . hedged on right and left by tall, closely planted poplars which lend the yard a secluded atmosphere'. This represents effectively Joe Keller's success in cocooning himself in a home cut off from the outside world, the inexorable intrusion of which is the play's main theme. Willy Loman cannot thus isolate himself domestically. Less successful and less affluent than Keller, he cannot live secludedly 'in the outskirts of an American town' but, as the light comes up on the set, 'we see a solid vault of apartment houses around the small, fragile-seeming home' and of these we are kept relentlessly aware until the final curtain. The threatening pressures of the outside world will intensify the fragility of that home throughout the play until eventually they destroy it completely : one of those pressures is embodied in the difficulties, all too familiar in the modern world, of home-ownership in the face of increasing property-values. The point is made, almost over-neatly, by Linda's last words as the play ends : 'I made the last payment on the house today. Today, dear. And there'll be nobody home. We're free and clear. We're free. We're free'.

The irony and pathos of those lines are prepared for throughout the play not only by the action but visually as well. The house is as much of a character in the play as the farmhouse had been in Eugene O'Neill's *Desire under the Elms* in 1924, and Miller adapted to his own ends that stage-set of the house in cross-section seen in its external surroundings. This 'exploded house' set which keeps the whole interior continuously on display mirrors the family combustion that came more and more to dominate the American theatre, and is peculiarly suited to this dramatic idiom. Its stylised unnaturalness reminds us that we are in a theatre — we can see actions happening simultaneously, and often quite independently, in two places — while its revelatory intimacy and disruption of privacy ensure our engagement in the action. We can be within and without simultaneously.

In the theatre Willy Loman's house is dwarfed by the omnipresence of the towering apartment houses all round it which, like O'Neill's elms, are a visual equivalent to the terrible claustrophobia of the play's theme. In a burst of misplaced agrarian escapism Willy goes out with a flashlight to sow the seeds that he has somehow never found time to plant before. On a bare stage this might seem insufferably allegorical : with the setting Miller demands, this consideration is overwhelmed by the painful grotesqueness of the situation. Nothing brings out more sharply the pathetic ineffectualness and bewilderment and littleness of the man than this scene, and the setting gives an added dimension to his otherwise petulant explosion : 'Where the hell is that seed? You can't see nothing out here. They boxed in the whole goddam neighbourhood'. [p.101]

The walls to which Willy is a prisoner are less tangible than

45

any of brick and stone, and yet by keeping us visually aware of those physical walls Miller simultaneously suggests the metaphysical walls as well. As the action of the play, taking place in Willy's mind, with effortless fluidity breaks through the walls of the stage house, the strength of the walls of his neurosis is accentuated. In the same way, in *Focus,* Lawrence Newman (whose place of work is the Wall Street district) had sat in a glass-walled private office, a prisoner to inner terrors of which the transparent walls make him and us the more conscious.

It is, in short, a mistake to apply too strictly to *Death of a Salesman* the standards of realism by which the earlier plays ask to be judged. That we are never told the nature of the merchandise Willy sells or the surnames of any of the characters other than the Lomans is not a failure of the realistic method. Miller's own answer, 'When asked what Willy was selling . . . I could only reply, "Himself" ' — is fair enough; these details are not necessary to a play that is nearer to expressionism than to realism.

(4)

In notices of the original production praise for Jo Mielziner's set was more general than for the structure of the play which puzzled many reviewers. One thought 'the episodic time-switching and place-switching' was a concession to audiences who really preferred the cinema; another sneered that 'it makes for easy play writing : problems of construction vanish'. More sympathetically a third wrote 'Usually I dislike seeing the whole of a house laid bare on the stage, but here imagination and good theatre-sense have triumphed' in the 'skeleton set and selective lighting'; although 'such juggling with time can be tiresome', in this case the 'frequent dips into the past are so smoothly managed that the main flow of the story towards its tremendous climax is never checked'. Yet even here there is a failure to remark the extent to which the effectiveness of both the set and the time-switching is due to their essential interdependence.

The naturalistic realism of the earlier plays would have been inappropriate. It would have been wrong to bring Willy's Chevrolet on to the stage for a polishing, even if Miller had been inclined to repeat the errors of *The Man Who Had All the Luck.* The car-polishing is recalled from the family past, not something happening in the dramatic present. That this is a play the main action of which is being seen by the audience through the mind of its central character cannot be too often emphasised. The shifts of Willy's consciousness shuttling on a loom of memory demand the maximum fluidity of movement, the minimum of scenery. The alternative of dispensing with scenery altogether had the precedent of *Our Town* to commend it, but Thornton Wilder's evocation of a New England town on the stage with the aid of a few chairs and a loquacious stage-manager had succeeded only because Grover's Corner was Everytown and did not need localising. Willy Loman's house is not as universal, nor is Willy Everyman. As Miller himself once tartly observed 'Well, it's obvious that Willy Loman can't be an average American man, at least from one point of view; he kills himself'.[19] Spatially the house is individualised as Willy's mortgaged property; temporally it is haunted by the ghosts of his localised past.

To speak of the action containing flashbacks is to miss its point; for 'flashbacks' I would prefer to substitute the more cumbersome but more accurate phrase 'scenes of recall'. Moreover, the sequence in which they are recalled is not chronological, random, or wholly consciously controlled by Willy. I have seen it suggested that the scene with the woman in the hotel bedroom is deferred until the end in order to give momentum and sensation to the flagging action. It has, however, been so patently prepared for in earlier scenes that to only the most naive spectator will it come as any sort of shock. It is deferred to the end by Willy's unconscious, for it is the one piece of the past that he least wishes to recall, the one that he has most successfully repressed. When circumstances have forced him to face it in his conscious mind, the action is truly at an end, for no longer can Willy escape the recognition of his own responsibility for what has happened to his family, no longer can he conveniently transfer the blame to Howard, to society, to impecuniousness, or even to luck. To argue that in these days of relaxed social morals one minor marital infidelity hardly constitutes grounds for suicide is, paradoxically, to add weight to the theme in the context of this play : for Willy Loman it *is* enough. He has not only, as he sees it, betrayed Linda and Biff, he has betrayed himself. Hap Loman can, with cheerful irresponsibility, seduce the fiancées of executives : the moral code by which Willy wants to live is significantly different from the one in which he has tried to bring up his sons. It is in this sense that Biff can call him a phony or, with greater tolerance, suggest that 'He had the wrong dreams. All, all wrong'. Coming near to recognising this himself at the end, however, Willy can still turn to suicide in the pathetically mistaken belief that it will strengthen his family's gratitude to him.

What I am saying about the play's structure has been said with some authority in the language of another discipline. Within eight months of its opening on Broadway a neuro-psychiatrist had published an encomium of it as :

> Visualised psychoanalytic interpretation woven into reality ... [a] masterful exposition of the unconscious motivations in our lives. It is one of the most concentrated expressions of aggression and pity ever to be put on the stage.[20]

By some of the details of the argument the layman may be unconvinced (the play as 'an irrational Oedipal blood-bath', the dinner to which Willy is invited as a totem-feast in which 'the sons recognise the father's authority and sexual rights', and Willy's departure to the cloakroom as 'castration-panic'), but its emphasis on the importance of the hallucinatory memory-sequences recognises one of the play's original contributions to dramatic structure :

> The past, as in hallucination, comes back to him; not chronologically as in 'flash-back', but *dynamically with the inner logic of his erupting volcanic unconscious.* In psychiatry we call this 'the return of the repressed', when a mind breaks under the invasion of primitive impulses no longer capable of compromise with reality.

The interweaving of past and present in this play succeeds, of course, because of the organic relevance of the remembered episode to Willy's present situation. However unfamiliar Miller may claim to have been with Freudian psychology, he has certainly developed the motivating 'inside-of-his-head' idea so smoothly and unobtrusively as to give the play a dramatic coherence more pleasing and more compulsive than his earlier more conventionally well-made plays had had.

(5)

It is, of course, a play about a man and his sons, about what we have since come to call 'the generation gap'; Miller, however, is careful not only to avoid moral judgments himself, but also to discourage us from moral judgments by not taking sides and by leaving deliberately vague and unverifiable many aspects of the Loman family's past and present.

Eric Bentley asks :

> Are the sons of Willy *seen* with the eye or just constructed from the *idea* that the present generation is 'lost'? Is Uncle Charlie [*sic*] of Alaska more than a sentimental motif? Is Willy's marriage *there* for us to inspect and understand down to its depths?

To each of these questions the answer is that these things are seen subjectively and developed only as far as Willy himself is capable of taking them. Only twice does Miller attempt to provide a brief external commentary, and to have used any character in a role comparable to that of Alfieri in *A View from the Bridge* would falsify the whole play : we must see Willy's story as Willy sees it.

This is not, however, to encourage the reader to identify himself with Willy or with any other character. The author concentrates on the diversity of forces at work and wants his audience to retain the capacity for objective judgment rather than for emotional identification. At the same time it has an expressionistic aspect in its concern with the external world as perceived by the mind of the dreamer; although it does not carry the distortion and fragmentation of that image to the lengths usually associated with expressionism. This mixture of methods does not work out completely successfully in the theatre, for a confusion of response is almost inevitable. That it should have been attempted at all is evidence of a theatrical adventurousness that is itself a sign of health.

Its appeal to the ordinary theatre-goer on both sides of the Atlantic is also a measure of Miller's success, even though some of its admirers may tend to sentimentalise it. Willy himself is a sentimentalist, particularly where the past is concerned, but the sentimentality that is in that respect a necessary element might have been a little more effectively distanced, especially in the 'Requiem'. The problem here is Linda. With none of the pathetic obsessions of Kate Keller and without the streak of unreasoning malice that Kate exhibits toward Ann, Linda is just too good for Willy and thus too good for the play. I do not mean that Linda is idealised; she is the most decently moral member of the family, but her devotion and loyalty to Willy are slightly over-emphasised and over-articulated. In the 'Requiem' it is her emotion more than its cause to which we respond, because she is herself confused about its cause. The Willy for whom she weeps is not worth her tears for what he is, so much as for what he might have been, and although our vicarious experience of sadness is a normal enough response to another's bereavement, in this case it is obscuring for us the perspective that the play should have sustained. Linda's tears are for humanity, Biff is talking about an individual, Happy is striking an attitude, while Charley is extemporising on an idea. All are characteristic reactions to the situation, and their very diversity is in keeping with the sense of multiplicity that the play has established. The difficulty is that an audience, instinctively expecting a summing-up, fastens on the dominant note, which is Linda's grief, and identifies itself with it. The fault is not entirely Miller's, although in a moment of self-criticism he confessed 'My weakness is that I can create pathos at will. It is one of the easiest things to do'.[21]

It is also in part the outcome of his moral earnestness, for earlier in the play he has used Linda as a mouthpiece with a lack of subtlety that has often been commented on (though sometimes exaggerated). This occurs at a culminating point of Act I, and, being the one scene in that act which does not take place inside Willy's head, gains an added air of objective reality. The whole scene ought to be judged in its context, but one part of one speech insists on isolating itself:

> I don't say he's a great man. Willy Loman never made a lot of money. His name was never in the paper. He's not the finest character that ever lived. But he's a human being, and a terrible thing is happening to him. So attention must be paid. He's not to be allowed to fall into his grave like an old dog. Attention, attention must be finally paid to such a person. [p.44]

The 'attention' that she demands for him is out of proportion to the situation; it seems to be an attention more penetrating, more far-reaching, than can reasonably be expected of his sons (from whom, anyway, she is really demanding sympathetic understanding, not attention). Mary McCarthy comments on 'the shrill, singsong voice of the mother':

> She is really admonishing the audience that Willy is, as she says, 'a human being'. But that is just it; he is a Human Being without being anyone, a sort of suffering Statistic. The mother's voice raised in the

50

old melancholy Jewish rhythms ('Attention must be paid' is not a normal American locution; nor is 'finally', placed where it is; nor is 'such a person' used as she uses it) seems to have been summoned from some other play that was about particular people.

The implication that this would have been a better play had Miller rooted it it more firmly in a Jewish milieu makes an attractive hypothesis, especially in the light of the success of Bernard Kops and Arnold Wesker in Britain a little later. Miss McCarthy argues that Willy 'could not be Jewish because he had to be American'. Miller had a better reason than this : a markedly Jewish Willy Loman might have made the play seem an attack on covert anti-Semitism in American business. By making Willy ethnically neutral Miller emphasises his point that Willy's trouble is that he is Willy in a particular society, not that he is a Jew, or a salesman, or a representative of any other group. In this one speech he is being presented as, in Miss McCarthy's words :

> A subject for the editorial page, which could take note of his working conditions, ask for unemployment benefits and old-age care for him, call 'attention' in short, to the problems of the salesman in the Welfare State.

But Linda's speech throws into too high a relief something which is only one part — and that not the main — of a play more complex than it seems.

Of *Our Town* Miller once remarked : 'I think that if the play tested its own theme more remorselessly, the world it creates of a timeless family and a rhythm of existence beyond the disturbance of social wracks would not remain unshaken.'[22] This more remorseless testing of the theme is what *Death of a Salesman* attempts, and the sentimentality that Linda brings to it really comes from the 'timeless family' and the 'rhythm of existence' of *Our Town*. Linda is the one character in this play who ought to have been developed more fully because of her importance in the two scenes that do not take place inside Willy's head. As it is, she is too much 'The Mother' and not enough an individualised Linda Loman.

(6)

Miller's comment on *Our Town* is offered in amplification of this proposition : 'Every form, every style, pays its price for its special advantages. The price paid by *Our Town* is psychological characterisation forfeited in the cause of the symbol'. The price paid by *Death of a Salesman* might be said to be psychological characterisation misunderstood in the audience's eagerness for a symbol and in their confusion over the form. The Cobb interpretation of Willy would have made him more of an individual, less of the Everyman, but, perhaps because of human sympathy for underdogs, the 'little man' image and the victim symbol seem to have predominated.

Perhaps the structure of the play does not make clear early enough the subjective angle from which Willy is being viewed; it begins so much like a realistic play that we have come to accept it as such before the first memory-sequence occurs, and we are not quick enough to see it as 'the inside of his head'. Yet if we will accept Willy as a character rather than a symbol or an abortive attempt at a tragic hero, some of the play's problems can better be kept in perspective. Even Mary McCarthy is prepared to allow some greatness to her 'suffering Statistic' for she, like Philip Hope-Wallace, sees in him analogies with King Lear, but also has some reservations : 'Lear, however, has the gift of language, which is not just a class-endowment, for the Fool has it too. This gift of language is what makes him human and not just "a human being" '. Shakespeare writing *King Lear,* however, is under no obligation to make an ancient Briton or his Fool speak like the seventeenth-century audience watching them. A twentieth-century audience could not be expected thus willingly to suspend its disbelief if a twentieth-century salesman used an idiom so markedly different from its own. Whether the action takes place inside or outside his head, the language must be realistic; whether he is Cobb's 'man rejoicing in his enormous vitality' or Muni's 'sad little chap beaten from the start', he is confused in his aspirations and certainly no more articulate than are those around him. If in *All My Sons* the characteristic idiom is the unanswered question, in *Death of a Salesman* it is the cliché worn so smooth as to limit communication to the superficial and the unimportant. Poetry in the language would be inappropriate, except to the extent that an occasionally heightened phrase acquires memorability. The poetry is in the characterisation and the theme. When, in the exceptional speech, Linda's idiom is heightened, it is heightened into the public statement. 'No one could write an editorial calling attention to the case of King Lear', says Mary

McCarthy with justice, but it is this speech with its rhetoric, not the play as a performed whole, that approaches the editorial. Yeats's distinction may be helpful : 'We make out of our quarrel with others rhetoric' (which is what Linda's speech does), 'but out of our quarrel with ourselves, poetry'. Though he does not fully recognise it, Willy is engaged throughout the play in a quarrel with himself, and out of it comes a kind of poetry, muted and non-Shakespearian, but by no means contemptible. Only to the extent that it echoes 'the still, sad music of humanity' does it make Willy a symbol of the human condition.

4

The Crucible

(1)

Many admirers of *Death of a Salesman* thought its successor, *The Crucible,* disappointingly less adventurous and innovatory; some found it too much of a morality play, while for others the parallel it suggested with American political events of their own day was an embarrassment; its structure, characterisation and language all came under attack. Yet in 1964 Herbert Blau could write 'Even to this day, a revival of *The Crucible* will take up slack at the box office' and in 1972 it was described as having been 'in almost continuous production in [the United States] and abroad' since its first Broadway revival had run for nearly three times as many performances as the original production.[23] In Britain it continues to enjoy a popularity in the theatre attributable only in part to its reputation in the classroom and even less to its oblique commentary on American political investigations in the 1950s.

At least two other plays on the Salem witches reached the stage before *The Crucible* opened on Broadway on 22 January 1953. One of them, Florence Stevenson's *Child's Play,* had been performed at Oklahoma Civic Playhouse in the previous November and at Swarthmore Little Theatre in December, as well as winning the Frederick Warde prize at the Theater-Americana in California. The other, by Louis O. Coxe (who had dramatised *Billy Budd* for Broadway presentation), was called *The Witchfinders,* and I remember seeing it in a studio-theatre production at the University of Minnesota at about the same time : the coincidental similarity of its subject-matter to that of *The Crucible* deterred Coxe from taking it further, but in other circumstances it would probably have done well.

One of the factors behind this revival of interest was no doubt the appearance in 1949 of Marion L. Starkey's *The Devil in Massachusetts,* a very readable investigation into the whole issue from the psychological as well as from the historical standpoint, which had made accessible a detailed account of the happenings and the trials. In her Introduction the author tells us that 'the story of 1692 is of far more than antiquarian interest; it is an allegory of our times. One would like to believe that leaders of the modern world can in the end deal with delusion as sanely and courageously as the men of old Massachusetts dealt with theirs'. She speaks of the 'ideological intensities which rent its age no less than they do ours,' and reminds us that : 'Only twenty witches were executed, a microscopic number compared to . . . the millions who have died in the species of witch-hunts peculiar to our own rational, scientific times'. By the autumn of 1952 these words had been given greater immediacy by the mounting fury of the latest species of witch-hunt being conducted by Senator Joseph McCarthy and by a Congressional investigation into un-American activities.

Here was an important subject ready to hand for an able dramatist to exploit, and Miller's background of Depression-engendered liberalism, his passionate belief in social responsibility and his preoccupation with themes of guilt all qualified him for it. We hardly need his specific assurance that he 'had known of the Salem witch hunt for many years before "McCarthyism" had arrived'; more illuminating is his passing reference to two of his earliest 'desk-drawer' plays: ' . . . a play about two brothers caught on either side of radicalism in a university, then a play about a psychologist's dilemma in a prison where the sane were inexorably moving over to join the mad'. Though the former may have been interesting as an early appearance of the Miller 'two brothers' pattern, no revision of either play would have dramatised as effectively as *The Crucible* the problems of 1952. The objection that Salem does not present a sufficiently precise parallel, because 'whereas witchcraft was pure delusion, subversion is a reality, no matter how unwisely or intemperately it may be combatted,'[24] ignores Miller's implication that, where evidence is only circumstantial, the dividing line between delusion and reality is difficult to draw.

It also confuses the main issue of Miller's play, towards which he had been moving in adapting *An Enemy of the People*. This had attracted him because it dealt with

. . . the central theme of our social life today. Simply, it is the question of whether the democratic guarantees protecting political

55

> minorities ought to be set aside in time of crisis. More personally, it
> is the question of whether one's vision of the truth ought to be a
> source of guilt at a time when the mass of men condemn it as a
> dangerous and devilish lie. It is an enduring theme ... because there
> never was, nor will there ever be, an organized society able to
> countenance calmly the individual who insists that he is right while
> the vast majority is absolutely wrong.[25]

By treating this problem in a seventeenth- rather than in a
twentieth-century context, Miller sacrifices the questionable
advantage of extreme topicality for the greater gain of
perspective. The terms in which he defines his anxiety widen
still further the theme's applicability : 'I saw accepted the
notion that conscience was no longer a private matter but one of
state administration. I saw men handing conscience to other
men and thanking other men for the opportunity of doing so'.
By now *The Crucible* is best discussed as an historical play on a
subject perennially topical and not exclusively American.

(2)

Miller provides a note on the historical accuracy of *The Crucible*
which indicates the care he has taken over it, and reference to
Marion Starkey's account or to the primary sources will quickly
substantiate this. (As many as possible of the original
documents bearing on the events and the trials were collated in
a three-volume typescript in Essex County in 1938; that this was
a Works Progress Administration project provides yet another
instance of the influence — unexpected, belated, and indirect
this time — of the Depression on Miller's work.)

Reference to one primary source, for example, *A Modest
Inquiry into the Nature of Witchcraft,* written in 1697 by John
Hale will demonstrate an obvious identity between Miller's
character in *The Crucible* and the man who wrote at the time : 'I
observed in the prosecution of these affairs, that there was in
the Justices, Judges and others concerned, a conscientious
endeavour to do the thing that was right'. Nevertheless, he is
not easy in his own conscience, though what he questions is
legal procedure rather than witchcraft itself : 'We may hence
see ground to fear that there hath been a great deal of innocent
blood shed in the Christian World, by proceeding upon unsafe
principles, in condemning persons for Malefick Witchcraft'.
Hale is, however, still convinced that witchcraft may exist and

that vigilance must be maintained : 'Seeing we have been too hard against supposed Malefick Witchcraft, let us take heed we do not on the contrary, become too favourable to divining Witchcraft [i.e. fortune telling]'.

The note of uncertainty, of suspended judgment, is very close to the keynote of *The Crucible,* which I find in the constant recurrence, on the lips of many different characters, of the phrase 'I think'. Much of the play could be summarised in Yeats's lines :

> The best lack all conviction, while the worst
> Are full of passionate intensity.

It is not so much a story of two ideologies in conflict as a story of conscientious endeavour in an uncertain world. This emerges with particular force and clarity in Act II, in, for example, such exchanges as this, in which Elizabeth Proctor tells her husband what she has heard from Mary Warren :

ELIZABETH: The Deputy Governor promise hanging' if they'll not confess, John. The town's gone wild, I think. She speak of Abigail, and I thought she were a saint, to hear her . . .

PROCTOR: Oh, it is a black mischief.

ELIZABETH: I think you must go to Salem, John. I think so. You must tell them it is a fraud. [pp. 53-54]

Joe Keller had asked in vain for guidance : no one could give it to him. Willy Loman's bewilderment at Charley, who had never told his son what to do, is the bewilderment of the man who has confidently inculcated in his own sons a complete set of values that have turned out to be wrong (just as Ben's advice to Biff, 'Never fight fair with a stranger, boy', is, in its context, implicitly criticised). In *The Crucible* the wiser characters do not presume to dictate any one's duty to him, for that would be asking him to hand over his conscience. Moreover, they themselves are too perplexed by the conflicting implications of the issues to be dogmatic. Elizabeth's quietly-delivered suggestions here are the thoughts of a worried but honest mind spoken aloud for her husband's benefit, and he replies in the same key: 'I'll think on it . . . I think it is not easy to prove she's a fraud, and the town gone so silly'. Far from indicating a limited vocabulary, either of character or author, the repetition of this formula 'I think' is in fact a very skilfully-managed way of suggesting the scruples, the misgivings, and the conscientious earnestness which are all that these people can bring against the diabolic impetus of the witch-hunt. It is significant that Miller chose to dramatise the story of John Proctor, the plain farmer, rather than the equally well-documented story of George Burrough, the minister, who was also accused of witchcraft and hanged for it. Miller's invention of Proctor's earlier adultery with Abigail is not the outcome of a mercenary desire to add a spice of sensationalism to the play. It is a similar insistence on the human vulnerability of a man who is not a saint, not even an ordained minister fortified by a theological training, but just a decent man trying to understand and to translate into action the dictates of his conscience, trying to do, not what he *feels*, but what he *thinks* is right.

(3)

In this concern with conscience and in other respects, too, *The Crucible* is the most Shavian of Miller's plays. The lengthy prefatory comment on the background, the postscript tracing the subsequent history of the characters, and the interrupting of dialogue (particularly in the first scene) for elaborations on the theme which are in no sense stage directions — all these recall Shaw. Miller had done something similar for a paperback *Death of a Salesman* issued in New York by Bantam Books in 1951, but in *Collected Plays* and other reprints he has reverted to the original text of that play. Thematically *The Crucible* is a play for Puritans in Shaw's, as well as in the more historically literal sense and it may to advantage be thought of in comparison with *Saint Joan*. Not only is each a religious-historical play culminating in an impressive trial scene followed by the martyrdom of the main character, but towards the end of both the tension is heightened by a dramatic *peripeteia* in which the prisoner, having made a 'confession' to escape death, suddenly realises the implications of it and recants by tearing the document to pieces.

In one important way they are more closely parallel than Miller's later discussion of *The Crucible* (in the Introduction to *Collected Plays*) might lead us to expect. There, referring to his sources, he speaks of the attitude of the authorities :

I do not think that either the record itself or the numerous commentaries upon it reveal any mitigation of the unrelieved, straightforward, and absolute dedication to evil displayed by the judges of these trials and the prosecutors. After days of study it became quite incredible how perfect they were in this respect. [pp. 42-43]

Shaw, on the other hand, is at pains to emphasise in his Preface that, at Joan's trial, the members of the court were 'far more self-disciplined and conscientious . . . than any English judge ever dreams of being in a political case in which his party and class prejudices are involved'; he dramatises them as acting honestly, rationally, coolly, and in strict accordance with their own beliefs. The only exception to this is the English chaplain, John de Stogumber, who is the bigot, the fanatic, and, above all, the self-deceiver who has allowed his principles to be overwhelmed by his passions, but even he cannot be said to be dedicated to evil.

The nearest parallel in *The Crucible* to de Stogumber is the Reverend Parris : both men's misplaced zeal makes them not only ridiculously quick to see insults to the dignity of the court in remarks by which their betters are undisturbed, but also vindictive and severe in questioning witnesses and in their reluctance to have any charge, however trivial, omitted. Parris's quarrels with Proctor and the villagers over the respect and the emoluments due to him indicate a similar small-mindedness, but this makes him more contemptible than evil. They are both little men. When de Stogumber refuses the Inquisitor's command to sit down, the Inquisitor blandly ensures his compliance by giving him permission to remain standing. Miller uses exactly the same device in Act II when the fractious Mary Warren resents being ordered to bed by Proctor [p.59]. In Act IV de Stogumber again comes to mind when Hale belatedly recognises the terrible consequences of his zeal : in similar circumstances the English chaplain gives way to abject hysteria and Hale, although he is more intelligent and more self-controlled, verges on the hysterical in his cry to Danforth, 'There is blood on my head! Can you not see the blood on my head?'[p.114]. When he goes on to urge Elizabeth to persuade her husband to save his life by lying he too allows emotionalism to swamp principle : 'Cleave to no faith when faith brings blood. It is a mistaken law that leads you to sacrifice' is advice that abdicates the responsibility for which the whole play pleads. Hale, like de Stogumber, cannot realise fully the implications of his own actions until he sees them embodied in the suffering of others but this comes from human weakness, not from a dedication to evil.

Such a dedication may be imputed in this play — and we may disregard the sources in this discussion — perhaps to those characters who deliberately and cynically give false evidence, or incite others to do so, for their own personal gain or gratification. This means Thomas Putnam with his greed for land, and Abigail with her lust for Proctor. Putnam, however, is only a minor character and Miller himself seems in two minds about the extent to which Abigail is evil or merely deluded. Evil can with much less certainty be imputed to Danforth and Hathorne who, hard and cruel as they may seem by our more enlightened standards, and even culpably credulous, are trying to arrive at a judgment on the basis of evidence quite outside their previous experience. They are bigoted fanatics, self-important, and without the intellectual distinction of Shaw's Inquisitor, but in performance they do not come over as positively motivated by evil. Yet Miller sees them in that light and has said categorically, that, were he to re-write what he regards as already 'a "tough" play', he would make it tougher by accentuating this evil still more :

> I believe merely that, from whatever cause, a dedication to evil, not mistaking it for good, but knowing it as evil and loving it as evil, is possible in human beings who appear agreeable and normal. I think now that one of the hidden weaknesses of our whole approach to dramatic psychology is our inability to face this fact — to conceive, in effect, of Iago. [*Collected Plays* p.44]

As a general principle, related to the practice of twentieth-century playwrights, this pronouncement could stimulate a very useful discussion. In the context of *The Crucible,* however, it is much more open to question, for to make the judges more evil would be to destroy by distortion one of the virtues of the play in the form in which we know it.

Its very considerable power in the theatre derives from its revelation of a mounting tide of evil gaining, in an entire society, an ascendancy quite disproportionate to the evil of any individual member of that society. What is so terrifying is to watch the testimony of honest men bouncing like an indiarubber ball off the high wall of disbelief that other men have built around themselves, not from ingrained evil, but from over-zealousness and a purblind confidence in their own judgment. What meaning has proof when men will believe only what they want to believe, and will interpret evidence only in the light of their own prejudice? To watch *The Crucible* is to be overwhelmed by the simple impotence of honest common sense against fanaticism that is getting out of control, and to be painfuly reminded that there are situations in which sheer goodness ('mere unaided virtue' in Melville's telling phrase) is just not enough to counter such deviousness.

In this respect, too, it will remain a more important indictment of McCarthy's America than would a more partisan piece. The real ugliness of that affair was not the megalomanic aspirations of a cynical demagogue but the appalling ease with which his methods achieved results. A force of evil of which ordinary men and women were the unintentional agents and the unrecognising victims, its moral damage was more serious to those who accepted it than to those who fought it or were victimised by it. In the Introduction to *Collected Plays* Miller brings this out very movingly by his anecdotes of the investigations, and then obscures it by his retrospective attribution of a greater evil to the individual judges of Salem than the play suggests. *The Crucible,* of course, was written before Miller's own clash with the Congressional Committee, and may therefore be somewhat less biased than the later Introduction.

In the theatre what comes across forcefully as the play's moral is the very Shavian one that in the life of a society evil is occasioned less by deliberate villainy than by the abnegation of personal responsibility. That is why Elizabeth quietly rejects as 'the Devil's argument' Hale's impassioned plea to her to help Proctor save himself : 'Life, woman, life is God's most precious gift; no principle, however glorious, may justify the taking of it'. Elizabeth, like Shaw's Joan, has learnt through suffering that 'God's most precious gift' is not life at any price, but the life of spiritual freedom and moral integrity. She replies to Hale in the play's idiom : 'I think that be the Devil's argument'. She believes this, but she cannot prove it : 'I cannot dispute with you, sir; I lack learning for it'. Again, as in *Saint Joan,* the learning of the scholars, the theologians, and the rulers is discredited, but not defeated, by the simple faith of a country woman.

The communication of this faith is Miller's best technical achievement in this play, for it depends very largely on his command of a new form of language adapted to its demands. Just as *Saint Joan* is the most poetic of Shaw's plays, so the language of *The Crucible* is heightened in exactly similar ways. However, where Shaw gives Joan a country dialect chiefly for anti-romantic and comic-realistic effect ('Where be Dauphin?' and 'Thou art a rare noodle, Master'), the rustic-archaic speech of Miller's characters gives them such a natural eloquence and simple dignity that he does not need to abandon it as Shaw does in the more highly-charged situations but can use it to good purpose throughout. It is simple and unpretentious, relying mainly on unusual forms of the verb and on 'Mister' as a form of address that becomes unexpectedly successful in conveying an unsophisticated kind of antagonistic formality. That it is not necessarily historically accurate is unimportant. In the theatre its quaintness is less noticeable than is its self-aware carefulness which strikes the keynote of the play, that of conscientious endeavour in an uncertain world.

There is a forthrightness about *The Crucible* that is as well supported by its language as by its structural simplicity. Miller has commented :

> I was drawn to this subject because the historical moment seemed to give me the poetic right to create people of higher self-awareness than the contemporary scene affords. I had explored the subjective world in *Salesman* and I wanted now to move closer to a conscious hero.

Willy Loman lacks the fullness of self-knowledge to which a tragic hero ought finally to come, and his death is an act of despair rather than of expiation, inevitable but falling short of cathartic grandeur. Proctor's stature is more heroic, but in calling him 'a conscious hero' Miller emphasises that his heroism is of less consequence than his consciousness. Thus, 'A point has to arrive where man sees what has happened to him. I think *The Crucible* is not more realistic but more theatrical than *Death of a Salesman*'. He also spoke of himself as 'trying to find a way, a form, a method of depicting people who do think'.[26] The recurrence of the idiom 'I think' indicates moral uncertainty on the part of the characters but also the conscientious ratiocination that has sought to resolve that uncertainty.

The heightening and formalising of the language, disliked by many of the original reviewers, is a step in the same direction. Six months after the play's New York opening Miller introduced some changes in the text, affecting particularly Proctor's part. In Act II, for example, it acquired greater lyricism from such lines as 'Lilacs have a purple smell. Lilac is the smell of nightfall, I think'. Similarly, in Act IV, his final speech to his wife had originally consisted simply of the exhortation 'Give them no tear! Show a stony heart and sink them with it!'; the revision made him answer Hale (whom he had previously ignored) and expanded the speech as follows :

HALE: Man, you will hang! You cannot!

PROCTOR *(his eyes full of tears)*: I can. And there's your first marvel, that I can. You have made your magic now, for now I do think I see some shred of goodness in John Proctor. Not enough to weave a banner with, but white enough to keep it from such dogs. *(Elizabeth, in a burst of terror, rushes to him and weeps against his hand.)* Give them no tear! Tears pleasure them! Show honor now, show a stony heart and sink them with it! [p.125]

Critics found the new version 'more fluid, forceful and poetic' but this particular change does more than merely enhance Proctor's eloquence at a moment of dramatic tension : by emphasising the self-knowledge he has achieved it deepens the play's impact as tragedy.

A number of additions were made to Act III at the same time. These are mostly in a lower key, but their general effect is to strengthen the blunt forthrightness with which Proctor stands up to Danforth's interrogation. Almost the whole of p.290 of the *Collected Plays* text (Penguin p.82), for example, was introduced in this way, and it establishes Proctor's candid straightforwardness as firmly as it illustrates his failure, at this stage of the action, fully to appreciate his vulnerability to the prejudice and deviousness of others. It comes hard to him to credit others with less integrity than he knows himself to possess.

It is sometimes suggested that the issue of the play would have been more clearcut had Miller not resorted to the Elizabeth/Abigail/Proctor triangle theme. Yet this is only one of the ways in which this play about thinking people insists that they are betrayed when thought is overruled by lust — lust for political power, for spiritual domination, for notoriety, for the property of others, and of course sexual lust. Moreover, Miller has always associated the crisis of public conscience with the private. When Proctor has been unfaithful to his wife (however disappointing their domestic life has become), how can she or we be confident of his ability to keep faith with his public and religious responsibilities? And, when he does keep faith with them, the knowledge of his earlier infidelity makes him more interesting as a character and his later victory more significant.

This element in the play gave Miller a good deal of trouble before he was satisfied with it. In particular, he introduced into his July 1953 revision of the play one new scene which he subsequently discarded. Inserted immediately before the present Act III, it takes place in a wood.[27] Proctor, on the eve of his wife's trial, meets Abigail to warn her of his intention to denounce her in court, unless she abjures her denunciation of witches. Abigail, however, half-crazed with religious mania and with frustrated love for Proctor (of which she reminds him passionately), does not believe him :

PROCTOR: . . . and you will never cry witchery again, or I will make you famous for the whore you are!

ABIGAIL *(she grabs him)*: Never in this world! I know you, John — you are at this moment singing secret Hallelujahs that your wife will hang!

PROCTOR *(throws her down)*: You mad, you murderous bitch!

ABIGAIL: . . . Fear naught. I will save you tomorrow. From yourself I will save you.

It is a powerful but quite superfluous scene, and its removal suggests that Miller is in two minds about Abigail. In this scene her religiosity makes her more pathetically deluded than evil, so that the second thoughts which led him to cut it out may be connected with the desire to accentuate the element of evil. The past relationship between Proctor and Abby has been clearly established in the first two acts; Proctor's eyes have been

The Crucible (Bristol Old Vic, 1954)

A View from the Bridge: Anthony Quayle (*Eddie:* right),
Mary Ure (*Catherine:* left), Megs Jenkins (*Beatrice:* centre)
(London, 1956)

A Memory of Two Mondays (New York, 1955)

opened to her true nature by the circumstances of his wife's arrest, after which he is hardly likely to seek a secret interview with her alone; and his disclosure of his intentions detracts from the dramatic power of the moment in Act III when he confesses his adultery. By the end of Act II our attention has been effectively directed to Proctor, and the spotlight of the action is already narrowing into focus on his eventual clash with the court, so that this wood scene is a distraction, as is also the opening passage of Act IV, with Tituba and Sarah Good.

Although Miller has not yet conquered his tendency to proliferate characters over-generously, he shows considerable skill in his manipulation and differentiation of them to develop the sense of a community. The only exception might be Francis Nurse, who is kept on the stage for a considerable part of Act II, and even more of Act III with nothing to do; no exit is marked for him in Act II, though he obviously leaves with Corey, and no cue for his entrance is given in Act III, though he is in the room when Danforth orders it to be cleared.[28] In the very earliest version of the play Miller seems to have reverted to the more extended manner of narration he was using before *All My Sons;* an opening scene set in a forest had to be abandoned because of the cost of building the set, but it is unlikely to have done much that is not better done in the final version by retrospective description. Something of the old realism still survives in some of the detailed settings and stage directions (at one point Danforth is even directed to blow his nose).

The stage directions are particularly explicit about the source of light in each scene. In Act I the sun streams through the leaded panes of a narrow window; in Act III sunlight pours through the two high windows; in Act IV, moonlight seeps through the bars of another high window. It shows how Miller sees the mood of the play — darkness and gloom penetrated by the single shaft of light cast by conscientiously dogged goodness. The revised version of July 1953, staged under Miller's own direction, 'did away with all scenery, and had the action take place against drapes and a light-flooded cyclorama'. The starkness of such a production would well suit the starkness of the play's theme, hovering on the brink of nihilism in a nightmare of lost innocence. 'If Rebecca Nurse be tainted, then nothing's left to stop the whole green world from burning' [p.67]. In simple phrases like this there is an eloquence of agony that makes this even more moving theatrically than *Death of a Salesman,* because there is no question of sentimentality. The Proctors' children, though mentioned, never appear. Our pity is demanded for an adult world run mad. When Proctor turns on Hale, the plain ordinariness of his language, lit by an unexpected simile, a rhetorical repetition, and an inversion of the normal order of two adjectives, is all that is needed;

> Why do you never wonder if Parris be innocent, or Abigail? Is the accuser always holy now? Were they born this morning as clean as God's fingers? I'll tell you what's walking Salem — vengeance is walking Salem. We are what we always were in Salem, but now the little crazy children are jangling the keys of the kingdom, and common vengeance writes the law! [p.72].

Anything more high-flown would be out of place in this play, which insists so relentlessly on the precarious foothold of goodness in a world swept by a wind of evil blowing at hurricane force. The courage of Proctor's conviction, however, and the shaft of light that irradiates the tragic blackness of *The Crucible,* anticipate the later plays' greater faith in human potential.

5

Two New York Plays

(1)

Miller's next dramatic venture was a double bill of two one-act plays, *A Memory of Two Mondays* and *A View from the Bridge,* produced on Broadway in September 1955. The opening performance was unfortunate and unimpressive, as Miller himself admits; the run was shorter than any of his plays since his first (with the exception of the Ibsen adaptation); and it was listed by *Variety* as a financial failure. Unlike their predecessors (to which they are not, in their different way, inferior), neither won any prizes, although *A View from the Bridge* was included in *The Best Plays of 1955-56.*

Less well-known in Britain, *A Memory of Two Mondays* is the simpler of the two. Fourteen people are brought together during working hours in the New York automobile-parts warehouse where most of them have spent all their working lives. One, however, the eighteen-year-old Bert, is there only temporarily : the two Mondays of the title are separated by the time it takes him to earn enough money for his first year at college. It is through his memory that we are shown the warehouse, its occupants, and such action as the play has : although in reality an unspecified number of months have passed between the opening and the closing of the action, time is compressed in his memory and there is thus no need for formal division into scenes. The continuity of flow suggests the unity of Bert's experience, the time gap between the two Mondays being marked only by a brief soliloquy by him, followed by a semi-lyrical exchange with another character. Surprised that the play 'was seen as something utterly sad and hopeless as a comment on life', Miller argues that it shows Bert working his way out of 'this endless, time-less, will-less environment'. It is not Bert who stays in our mind, though, so much as the company in which he moves, and their aura of diminished hope.

67

Bert does nothing to further such action as there is; nothing is done to him in any violent sense; he is exposed to experience in a way that is at once lifelike and artistically satisfying in a Chekhovian manner. He sees significant change in two of the characters, Tommy and Kenny; another, Gus, loses his wife on the first Monday and himself dies on the second. The passage of time is hinted at by unobtrusive signs of ageing in all the characters in the second part; not only have they all calcified a little but Bert has matured in his view of them. Miller's theme here is, as in *All My Sons* and *Death of a Salesman*, the adjustment of the young person to the disillusions and compromises of adult life. Bert, like Biff and Happy, is at least young enough for this to be convincing, unlike Chris Keller: I suspect that many readers, looking back on *All My Sons*, share my surprise at the stage direction that puts his age at thirty-two, for he seems a good deal younger than that in his innocence.

Miller's own pre-college experience between 1932 and 1934 indicates an autobiographical basis for this deeply-felt and nostalgic piece of writing. It is the most dated of all his work: 'so much so', he confesses wryly, 'that many took it for granted it had been written a long time ago and exhumed'. As he says, 'the play speaks not of obsession but of rent and hunger and the need for a little poetry in life'. It is not 'utterly sad' but it is what Miller calls it, 'a pathetic comedy', and it evokes, in a way not easy to define, the atmosphere of the 1930s. Beyond a few passing and brief references to Hitler and Roosevelt it eschews the obvious and tedious documentation of topical allusion, relying instead on a delicate conveying of mood. Discretion or retrospect has eliminated any period propaganda and the pathetic is well kept in check by touches of humour. There is also a realistic grasp of human nature that goes beyond pathos. The personal ties that develop between people who are brought together only by their employment are shown with real insight. Their conversation is of baseball and the other minor consolations of living; there is sexual banter, facetiousness, coarseness, and not infrequently irritation, but only just beneath the surface there is genuine concern. The relationships between them are the most casual of any in Miller's plays and the play sets out to prove less than do the others, but, even while it insists on the transience and ultimate unsatisfactoriness of such relationships, it communicates an unusual sense of the warmth they can generate. Within its limited scope the character of Gus — bawdy, crude, sentimental, irascible, irresponsible, yet generous, kind-hearted, and with his own sense of values and loyalty — is one of Miller's richest achievements. The speech in which he traces his twenty-two years with the firm in terms of the car models he has outlived (*Collected Plays* p.370) is at once lifelike and in its own way poetic. A comparison with the Gus of *The Man Who Had All the Luck* would provide a quick and convenient index of Miller's progress as a dramatist in just over a decade.

A Memory of Two Mondays is clearly a minor play by a major playwright who has learnt to co-ordinate all the constituent elements into a unified pattern. Thus the counterpoise of the two halves of the play, already suggested by the title, is worked out simply but effectively by a see-saw relationship between two of the characters. Tommy, the drunken clerk of the first part, becomes by a tremendous effort of will the triumphant teetotaller of the second, while Kenny, at first a poetry-spouting, likeably tough Irish idealist, has by the second part begun the process of degeneration into a drunken lout, though flashes of the old decency still survive. His exchange with Bert, which forms the hinge between the two parts, prefigures this in the skill with which tone and language modulate from the poetic to the aggressive (*Collected Plays* pp.358-359). There is no direct causal connection between the changes that take place in Tommy and Kenny, they have no influence on each other, nor is there any significant interaction between them in the story. In the second part, however, we recognise a loss of vitality in both of them: the reformed Tommy has a priggish rectitude and a hardness that are much less attractive than his earlier, if unregenerate, warmth; and the Kenneth who has turned to drink as an anodyne has lost the rugged spontaneity that he had at first.

Other contrasted pairings in the play are readily discernible: Patricia the young girl discovering her sexuality and Agnes the older spinster capable of a more genuine affection; Raymond the manager, competent but 'weighed down by responsibilities, afraid to be kind', and Larry, living beyond his means and inclined to surliness, yet the real expert in the place. The scene in which the two men try to help a customer with a comically inadequate idea of the part that he wants (*Collected Plays* pp.350-351) is a neatly observed cameo and indicative of the difference between them. It is also an example of Miller's respect for the expert, in whatever walk of life.

The formal patterning of the play helps to suggest the exposure to experience that Bert is undergoing. The repetition of situations and the sequence of incidents in the two halves, the recurrence of similar snatches of conversation, and the sustained focal passivity of Bert, all establish this sufficiently, so that the little verse soliloquy that Miller allows him towards the end seems not only self-conscious but superfluous, except to the extent that self-consciousness is in keeping with Bert's adolescence. The movement, rhythm, and form of the play have brought out, quietly and without didacticism, the monotony of the warehouse existence and the difference between Bert and the rest: it does not need the elaboration of this coda, which compares badly with Gus's less pretentious roll-call of the automobiles of past years that immediately precedes it. The play does not call for this heightening of language as *The Crucible* did; though its mood is lyrical, its language need not be — indeed, ought not to be, because the realistic is as important an element in it as the lyrical. Both the unity of mood that it sustains and the passivity of its central figure dictate its shape: it is a play that can be too easily underestimated.

(2)

A View from the Bridge began as a one-act drama, Miller's original explanation being: 'I have made the assumption that the audience is like me and would like to see, for once, a fine, high, always visible arc of forces, moving in full view to a single explosion'.[29] The expansion of it into a two-act play was carried out for its London production. Giving his reasons for the change in *Collected Plays,* Miller does not mention the abandoning of the verse form into which much of the play was originally cast. Often this conversion was effected merely by resetting the original as prose without changing it in any other way. Thus Rodolpho's longer speeches at what is now the beginning of Act II were printed as verse (though Catherine answered in prose) but were verbally identical with the *Collected Plays* text. Elsewhere the changes were greater. The pattern of Alfieri's opening speech was entirely different. After

70

the prose description of his practice (from 'My wife has warned me . . .' to 'the petty troubles of the poor — and yet . . .') he continued :

> When the tide is right
> And the wind blows the sea air against these houses,
> I sit here in my office,
> Thinking it is all so timeless here.
> I think of Sicily, from where these people came,
> The Roman rocks of Calabria,
> Siracusa on the cliff, where Carthaginian and Greek
> Fought such bloody fights. I think of Hannibal,
> Who slew the fathers of these people; Caesar
> Whipping them on in Latin.
> Which is all, of course, ridiculous.
> Al Capone learned his trade on these pavements . . .

This is much less personal and more relaxed in its detachment than the prose version, where Alfieri's identification of himself as an Italian immigrant and his vision of 'another lawyer, quite differently dressed', hearing the same complaints in ancient Sicily, is better prepared for and more immediate in its impact. The parenthetic allusion to Al Capone as 'the greatest Carthaginian of all' really says more than does the versified ancient-history passage just quoted. There is also a repetitiveness about the verse, despite its occasional felicity :

> And yet, when the tide is right,
> And the green smell of the sea
> Floats through my window,
> I must look up at the circling pigeons of the poor,
> And I see falcons there,
> The hunting eagles of the olden time,
> Fierce above Italian forests . . .
> And as the parties tell me what the trouble is
> I see cobwebs tearing, Adriatic ruins rebuilding themselves; Calabria;
> The eyes of the plaintiff seem suddenly carved,
> His voice booming toward me over many fallen stones.

Though he was right to abandon it, this experimentation shows the innovative variation of style that is evidenced in all his plays.

Rewriting the play enabled Miller, as he himself says, to express more fully the viewpoints of Beatrice and Catherine, and thus to make Eddie less of a monster. How this greater realism is achieved may be seen by comparing the following passage of the original with the scene which, in *Collected Plays,* occupies pp.384-387(Penguin pp.18-21) :

EDDIE: Your do your lessons today, Garbo?

CATHERINE: Yeah; I'm way ahead anyway. I just gotta practice from now on.

BEATRICE: She could take it down almost as fast as you could talk already. She's terrific. Read something to her later, you'll be surprised.

EDDIE: That's the way, Katie. You're gonna be all right, kid, you'll see.

CATHERINE *(proudly)*: I could get a job right now, Eddie. I'm not even afraid.

EDDIE: You got time. Wait'll you're eighteen. We'll look up the ads — find a nice company; or maybe a lawyer's office or somethin' like that.

CATHERINE: Oh boy! I could go to work now, my teacher said.

EDDIE: Be eighteen first. I want you to have a little more head on your shoulders. You're still dizzy yet. *(To Beatrice:)* Where's the kids? they still outside?

BEATRICE: I put them with my mother for tonight. They'd never go to sleep otherwise. So what kinda cargo you have today?

In the expanded version Catherine has already been offered a job and she and Beatrice are breaking the news to Eddie. This heightens the dramatic effectiveness and rightly makes the role of Beatrice much more active. Realism is increased by the impression of the world outside that their discussion produces, and by the sense of a normal domestic relationship which is counterpointed by the mounting tension of the argument. The whole scene becomes more impulsive and emotional, and Eddie's objections, by being made less rational and plausible, become more ambivalently motivated; this is nicely brought out (p.386; Penguin pp.20-21) by his sudden change of heart and Catherine's impassioned response. Another small, but appropriate, change, by deleting the reference to the children, makes Eddie and Beatrice childless.

These changes improve the play, and the expansion into two acts does not diminish its 'fine, high, always visible arc of forces'. Synge might make a one-act tragedy out of *Riders to the Sea,* but the greater complexity of Miller's theme demands a more extended treatment.

The theme is an unusual one for Miller, and at first sight its preoccupation with incestuous desires and suspicions of homosexuality might suggest Tennessee Williams. It is almost as though, stung by such generalisations as Kenneth Tynan's — 'At a time when Miller's plays were growing colder and more intellectualised, Williams's blazed hotter and more sensuous' — he had deliberately challenged Williams on his own ground by writing about the Sicilian immigrants whose passionate obsessions in *The Rose Tattoo* had prompted Tynan's remark. This, however, is probably no nearer the truth than is Henry Popkin's suggestion that it was written 'with the evident intention of replying to Kazan', who had recently filmed Budd Schulberg's *On the Waterfront*. The social reference of Miller's play is at once far greater than Williams would want and far less political than Schulberg's. The betrayal of which Eddie is guilty is very different from the betrayal in *Waterfront* of a reformer by a hoodlum, and although Miller's enquiry into New York delinquency[30] might make a good play, that is not what this is about.

'The play's main topic', as Popkin says, 'has become Eddie's troubles.' Certainly sexuality is prominent among Eddie's troubles, but so it had been for John Proctor, without prompting comparisons between that play and Williams's work. That Eddie's troubles are domestic rather than, as Proctor's had been, predominantly public, and that Sicilians are characteristically more passionate than New England Puritans, only goes part of the way to differentiating the two plays. Proctor's infatuation with Abigail is over before the play begins (the removal of the scene in the wood emphasises this), whereas Eddie's problems are very much alive throughout the play. Proctor's infidelity is presented as morally wrong — in the context of the play, sinful; Eddie's difficulties are more confused — and to him more confusing — because they are largely unconscious and unconsummated. Yet there is, in *A View from the Bridge,* a highly-charged atmosphere of suppressed sexuality that erupts from time to time and with which all the moments of dramatic crisis are associated.

The contest of strength with which Act I ends is plainly a display of virility prompted in Eddie by the sexual implications of the dance between Catherine and Rodolpho that has preceded it. The use of 'Paper Doll' as a theme song in this act establishes ironically the sexual inaccessibility of Catherine to her uncle and the apparent sexual ambiguity of Rodolpho that, in Act II, leads Eddie to kiss him. In 1955, of course, so explicit an act on the stage had an impact far more sensational than it would ever have again. I do not, however, see it as necessarily proving that Eddie is sexually attracted to Rodolpho and yet horrified to realise it: his hostility to Rodolpho is adequately explained by Catherine's affection for him and by his apparent effeminacy. Yet Eddie is disturbed by aspects of his own sexuality that the events of the play disclose to him, and I find it especially significant that, when Marco kills him at the end, he does so with a cry, not of 'Traitor!' as one might expect, but of 'Anima-a-a-l!' Yet, important as sexuality undoubtedly is in *A View from the Bridge,* it is strongly counterpointed by another theme that is markedly un-Williams-like.

(4)

The choric role of Alfieri may recall Tom in *The Glass Menagerie:* in the first version he began by bidding the audience 'Good evening. Welcome to the theater', much as Tom's opening speech insists that this is a play, not a slice of life. But Alfieri is far more detached from this story than Tom is from his, and this marks the distinction between Williams and Miller. Alfieri represents both the secular and the moral law, the social forces that Eddie is to reject. He is the principle of social order that is always dominant in Miller's drama, and the added emphasis of his choric role sets 'Eddie's troubles' in a wider context. Another writer might have used a priest in this capacity, as Schulberg uses Father Barry to befriend his Irish-immigrant longshoremen, but Miller's choice of a lawyer is significant.

In *All My Sons* Ann's brother George is a lawyer, and so is Bernard in *Death of a Salesman.* Either could have gone into any other profession as far as the story is concerned, for all that is required of them is that they make good; indeed, it might have been better to have George in some other post, for a lawyer might be expected to handle the Keller situation more professionally and less emotionally than he does. But lawyers they are, as though Miller feels a particular symbolism of rightness in the law; for George, Bernard, and Alfieri, with

74

increasing prominence in each successive play, do stand for order and moral justice in a more than professional sense, and it is, of course, that order and moral justice which is betrayed by the theocracy in *The Crucible*. This point, to which I called attention in 1961, has since then been interestingly reinforced by the fact that Quentin in *After the Fall* is a lawyer and Victor, in *The Price*, also represents the law in the appropriately more humble role of policeman.

If, however, in these two later plays Miller seems less confident than he was of the efficacy of the law in ordering human affairs, this too is presaged in *A View from the Bridge*. Alfieri cannot avert the disaster that Eddie is bringing on himself, and he admits it in a phrase more revealing than it sounds :

> But I will never forget how dark the room became when he looked at me; his eyes were like tunnels. I kept wanting to call the police, but nothing had happened. Nothing at all had really happened. [p.65].

Miller's characters are always beyond the help of the police, because what happens to them is not actionable in any ordinary manner. *Focus* opens with an unknown woman calling 'Police!' in the night, while Mr Newman finds excuses for not intervening in what is not his affair. Another nocturnal disturbance from which he thinks to escape by simply phoning the police turns out to be something too trivial to call the police to, but all the more frightening because of that. Chris Keller cannot bring himself to call the police to his father: he announces that he will 'take him in', but instead gives his father the opportunity of suicide. The ordinary stable world of crime and punishment is always just around the corner in Miller's plays — within call, yet out of reach. These people are their own executioners in obedience to laws more inexorable than those of criminal justice.

This connects with another key phrase in Miller's work, one that Eddie uses with increasing vehemence in the closing minutes of this play: 'I want my name!' When John Proctor recants his confession he does so because he refuses to put his name to it; taxed with the illogicality of his position, he breaks out into an impassioned explanation: 'Because it is my name! Because I cannot have another in my life . . . How may I live without my name? I have given you my soul; leave me my name!' This name for which Proctor dies is his moral integrity, not merely his reputation with others, but reputation is an important aspect of it. Thus Abigail's jealousy of her good name in Salem received further emphasis in the revision of that play by the addition of the lines 'My name is good in the village! I will not have it said my name is soiled'. In *An Enemy of the People* Miller had made Morten Kiil similarly anxious that his name should be kept clean. Willy Loman distinguished, in one of the memorable phrases of *Death of a Salesman,* between being liked and being well liked, but Willy had the wrong values. Miller's preoccupation with the name as reputation and the name as moral integrity suggests another distinction, this time between being known and being wholly known. The reputation, the name that Willy, Kiil, and Abigail have, has some validity, but will not stand up to the fierce scrutiny that John Proctor's or Eddie Carbone's will. Miller commented, as long ago as 1949 :

> For, if it is true to say that in essence the tragic hero is intent upon claiming his whole due as a personality and if this struggle must be total and without reservation, then it automatically demonstrates the indestructible will of man to achieve his humanity.[31]

This certainly fits Proctor well: his whole due as a personality requires that he retain control of his own conscience and his own destiny.

Because reviewers missed the significance of this in *The Crucible,* Miller tells us, he determined to make it explicit in the next play: 'The engaged narrator, in short, appears'. It is only in the later version, however, that Alfieri really makes clear Eddie's 'will to achieve his humanity'. Originally the play had concluded thus :

Most of the time now we settle for half,
And I like it better.
And yet, when the tide is right
And the green smell of the sea
Floats in through my window,
The waves of this bay
Are the waves against Siracusa,
And I see a face that suddenly seems carved;
The eyes look like tunnels
Leading back toward some ancestral beach
Where all of us once lived

And I wonder at those times
How much of all of us
Really lives there yet,
And when we will truly have moved on,
On and away from that dark place,
That world that has fallen to stones?
This is the end of the story. Good night.

It is not surprising that one critic should have written: 'The play is almost glaringly primitivist, and in feeling operatic; the right analogy seems not with the Greeks but with Merimée, the Merimée not only of *Carmen* but of *Mateo Falcone*'.[32] The primitive element of the vendetta has already been adequately established by the fight, and Eddie's death constitutes a sufficient criticism of it without this added emphasis. What the re-written curtain speech does is to set the story, not in historical, but in moral perspective, and to lift it above the vendetta story by its insistence on Eddie's moral intransigence :

> Most of the time now we settle for half and I like it better. But the truth is holy, and even as I know how wrong he was, and his death useless, I tremble, for I confess that something perversely pure calls to me from his memory — not purely good, but himself purely, for he allowed himself to be wholly known and for that I think I will love him more than all my sensible clients. And yet, it is better to settle for half, it must be! And so I mourn him — I admit it — with a certain . . . alarm. [p.85].

This is emotive writing which will not be to everyone's taste, but by introducing the important phrases 'himself purely, for he allowed himself to be wholly known', this version prevents our dismissing Eddie as the animal that Marco has just called him. Alfieri is essential to this play, not because of the obtuseness of of the audience (as Miller seems to suggest), but because of the enormity of Eddie's offence against our normal social values. Except to the extent that Alfieri's 'certain alarm' with which he mourns Eddie recalls his earlier instinct to call the police, Miller's judgment of Eddie invites us temporarily to suspend our normal values. We see

> that however one might dislike this man, who does all sorts of frightful things, he possesses or exemplifies the wondrous and humane fact that he too can be driven to what in the last analysis is a sacrifice of himself for his conception, however misguided, of right, dignity, and justice.

77

Miller's insistence throughout his work on the individual's duty to his own conscience is widened here by the recognition that his conscience may mislead him. *A View from the Bridge* is tragic because of Eddie's integrity, sustained to his own destruction against the counsels of his friends and the code of his society. *Death of a Salesman* is not tragic because Willy Loman has no such conception of integrity. Eddie really is 'intent upon claiming his whole due as a personality'; he wants his respect (a key word on the lips of several characters here) and sacrifices everything to that.

This play is 'a view from the bridge' not only because it is set in the shadow of Brooklyn Bridge, but more importantly because it tries to show all sides of the situation from the detached eminence of the external observer. Alfieri is essential to the play because he is the bridge from which it is seen. (Budd Schulberg's title equally designates the more engaged angle from which he studies life 'on the waterfront'.) Miller's fondness for imagery of vision and perspective is evident from *Focus* right through his work. The two New York plays that formed this double bill are similarly connected. The transition from the first to the last Monday is effected by Bert and Kenneth with youthful optimism removing the grime of years from the warehouse windows because 'it'll be nice to watch the seasons pass'. The passing of the seasons, however, brings a change in the ownership of the premises opposite, and when a brothel is established there Kenneth's vestigial decency is stung into protesting to his manager: 'I mean to say, it's a terrible disorganizing sight staring a man in the face eight hours a day, sir.' The reply has the merit of logic: 'Shouldn't have washed the windows, I guess', but is used ironically by Miller.

The moral he really points has been criticised as over-obvious, but it is none the less relevant to a good deal of American drama. If you want to look at views from bridges, to explode the normal façade of a house to see what goes on inside, you must be prepared to accept what you see and to assess it for what it is, not for what you would like it to be. Cleaning windows to watch the seasons pass may bring a brothel into view as well, but there is no reason to concentrate on either to the exclusion of the other. *A View from the Bridge* may bring unexpectedly into focus the tragic integrity of Eddie

78

Carbone, but it does not minimise the enormity or the ugliness of his betrayal of his family.

To express the dualism of this view, Miller's dialogue, blending Eddie's Brooklyn vernacular with the more imaginative speech of Rodolpho and Alfieri, is better than the original poetic idiom would have been, because of its greater realism. The dramatic climaxes of this play do not rely on words, but are passions visualised in action. The intensity of action is often deliberately contrasted with the casualness of the dialogue, as in the sparring scene and the chair-lifting. No words could approach the effect in the theatre of the kiss which Eddie gives Rodolpho and which signals so startlingly his contempt for him. It is a breaking-out, a point of no return, comparable in its theatrical power to Serafina's shattering, in *The Rose Tattoo,* of the urn containing her husband's ashes, or, in a different key, to the window-cleaning in *A Memory of Two Mondays.* As with all Miller's plays, there is an effect of great power, of immediacy, and above all of a deeply-felt human concern. The skill of construction is once again allied to a dextrous manipulation of the dramatic lens so as to bring into focus two views of the same sequence of events, and the disciplined handling of elemental passions suggests new potentialities in Miller.

6

Taking Stock and Changing Direction

(1)

By the end of the 1950s, despite (and in some ways because of) the contretemps with Congress, Miller's eminence as a dramatist was beyond dispute. Honorary degrees and similar forms of public recognition began to multiply. On both sides of the Atlantic his plays were attracting serious critical attention.[33] Miller himself seemed to feel that he had reached a watershed. In 1957 he collected his plays into one volume, its definitiveness underlined by its fiftyfive-page critical introduction. In other essays he formulated explicitly and theoretically themes that had been implicit in his plays to date; 'The Family in Modern Drama' (1956) and 'On Social Plays' explored the connection between the family group and the larger grouping of society. By prefixing 'On Social Plays' to the 1957 text of *A View from the Bridge* he seemed to emphasise that piece's social relevance rather than its sexual aspects. His contribution to a *Tulane Drama Review* symposium in 1958 summed up his views on *Death of a Salesman*. On the American theatre in general he published, in *Harper's,* 'The Shadows of the Gods' (1958) and 'The State of the Theatre' (1960).

Drama, he concluded, had moved, in the 1950s, 'to a dangerous extreme of triviality', but he offered no neat remedy:

I am not calling for more ideology . . . I am simply asking for a theatre in which an adult who wants to live can find plays that will heighten his awareness of what living in our time involves. I am tired of a theatre of sensation, that's all. I am tired of seeing man as merely a bundle of nerves. That way lies pathology, and we have pretty well arrived.[34]

From the works so far discussed it is apparent that living in our time essentially involves for Miller the acquisition of the sense of community to which, in 'On Social Plays', he had attributed the success of Greek classical drama :

> The Greek citizen of that time thought of himself as belonging not
> to a 'nation' or a 'state' but to a *polis*. The polis were small units,
> apparently deriving from an earlier tribal organization, whose
> members probably knew one another personally because they were
> relatively few in number and occupied a small territory . . . The
> preoccupation of the Greek drama with ultimate law, with the
> Grand Design, so to speak, was therefore an expression of a basic
> assumption of the people, who could not yet conceive, luckily, that
> any man could long prosper unless his polis prospered.

The preoccupation with ultimate law in *A View from the
Bridge* and the vendetta element there may not unreasonably
be described as 'deriving from an earlier tribal organisation'.
The Italian immigrant longshoremen constitute a *polis* whose
members know one another personally, being few in number
and occupying a small territory. Eddie's loyalty to Marco and
Rodolpho as 'submarines' (unauthorised immigrants) is more
than a loyalty to his wife's relations: it is an ethnic loyalty to a
self-contained group with common antecedents. This is
emphasised by the anecdote of Vinny Bolzano, who betrayed a
'submarine' uncle, and by the two immigrant relatives of Lipari,
who have no direct role in the play, as well as by the almost
ritualistic attitude of 'a certain formal stiffness' that Marco tries
to preserve towards Eddie. Thus Eddie's betrayal of the
'submarines' is a threat to 'the right way to live *together*', which
Miller regards as the great feature of the *polis;* in cutting himself
off from his *polis* he destroys himself.

Joe Keller, Willy Loman, John Proctor and Dr. Stockmann
have also been separated from their larger and less ethnically-
determined *polis,* but like Eddie they have also by their actions
destroyed the unity of their immediate family. By posing the
question 'How can the larger society flourish if the smaller unit
of the family does not?' they illustrate the interrelatedness at
the heart of Miller's theory of the family and society. These are
all social plays, but because the breakdown of the family is the
most immediately apparent and most dramatically effective
aspect of them in the theatre, Miller's critical expositions may
have helped to clarify their larger implications.

(2)

A View from the Bridge was followed by a nine-year period

without a new Miller play. Instead his energies appeared to be directed into critical essays and short stories, one of which, 'The Misfits' (1957), was developed four years later into a filmscript. The differences between the two versions are interesting in their own right and also indicative of changes in outlook that are to affect his later dramas.

The original story was Hemingway-like in the concentration on a man's world that led *Esquire* to caption it 'The Last Frontier of the Quixotic Cowboy'. It seemed another addition to the established American genre of the hunting story and another lament for the dissolution of the American Dream. The cowboys, while responding to the wild beauty of the mountain scenery, constantly contrast with it a memory of the days when the frontier was wilder still and when the mustang herds were larger. Striking a balance between the falsely-tough and the facilely-sentimental, Miller tempers their nostalgic wonder with a real feeling of loss which is partly due to the passage of time, partly to the inadequacy of man to his opportunities, partly to the inability of deracinated man to make a home for himself in the world. The knowledge that the mustangs they are roping will be sold for canning as pet-food devalues their activity for them as much as for the reader. What sounds at the beginning like a celebration of sturdy masculine independence becomes by the end an indictment of the times and even of the men themselves, the misfits whose reiterated conviction that 'It's better than wages' partially obscures for them the sterility of their existence.

The young cowboy, Perce, is living the part of Biff Loman's life that is mentioned only briefly in *Death of a Salesman* when Biff tells his brother of his escape to the West and its failure to satisfy him :

> And whenever spring comes to where I am, I suddenly get the feeling, my God, I'm not gettin' anywhere! What the hell am I doing, playing around with horses, twenty-eight dollars a week! [p.16].

Perce is less agonised at this than Biff: ' "You know something, Gay? I'm never goin' to amount to a damn thing". Then suddenly he laughed'. Perce's companionship with the older misfit is denied to Biff, but both have guilty recollections of neglected family ties. These take Biff periodically back to the

Brooklyn home, but Perce can expiate his guilt by an occasional phone call.

Much of this survives in the film version, though Perce is slighty less central than in the story. His resemblance to Biff is intensified, when he phones his mother, by the hostile allusion to his father: 'Well, you married him, I didn't! Tell him hello for me'. (A similar echo of *Death of a Salesman* occurs when Guido, in drink and desperate isolation, starts ineffectually to repair the house exterior after dark and succeeds only in treading the flowers down.) Perce in the film, doggedly determined but inexpert in his rodeo performance, is as much a misfit as before, though less phlegmatic in his acceptance of the fact. If he is less dependent on Gay, and less inclined to hero-worship of him, this is only in part because he is more mature. Gay's role is also shifted further from the centre and a new loyalty weakens his ties to the younger man.

This change of emphasis, the most obvious difference between the two versions, is effected by the introduction into the film of a woman who had existed in the story only in the conversations of the men. In retrospect many film-goers will recall two things about *The Misfits:* the vitality of Roslyn and the cinematic excitement of the mustang hunt in which the film culminates. This is not to belittle the performance of Clark Gable in what was to be his last screen role, the ageing cowboy Gay; had the film given to his part the unrivalled centrality it had in the story he would have been equal to it, and I am not implying that Marilyn Monroe, as Roslyn, out-acted him. The strength of her performance here had been the weakness of some of her others, that she was simply herself. This part was written specifically for her and celebrated the qualities in her own personality that had attracted Miller. To this her physical beauty, successfully as the camera caught it, was subordinated or, at times, contrasted, but never unsympathetically.

Insecure, relatively inarticulate, and not over-intelligent, Roslyn is vitality incarnate. The scene in the bar, where she is concentrating on her dexterity with the paddle-ball, was skilfully shot so as to focus on her physicality and the grace of her movements as well as on the enthusiasm of the onlookers. The old lady moving with a collecting-box among them is used to reinforce Roslyn's life-giving energy by an ironic contrast: the funds she is raising are to be devoted to buying 'a fence around the graveyard, keep these cowboys from pasturing their horses on the graves'. Touches of humour like this and like the little boy's inadvertent swallowing of the spiked drink contribute further to the liveliness of the scene.

Earlier, dancing with Guido, Roslyn is told by him that his wife had no gracefulness. Uncomprehendingly, she asks 'Whyn't you *teach* her to be graceful?'; when Guido questions the possibility of doing that, she explains that 'if you loved her you could have taught her anything'. The naive sincerity of this is the emotional equivalent of her bodily movements — simple, flowing, natural and spontaneous. In a world where nature has been devalued, where mustangs are hunted for pet-food by men in trucks and aircraft, where, as Gay laments, 'it just got changed around, see?', Roslyn represents the few unchanging principles. She is the eternal woman, the embodiment of life, of hope, and of continuity. Innocent, trusting, tender, unsure of herself but sure of the possibilities of life, in sympathy with the natural world, inclined to sentimentality, she can easily be made to sound like the idealised dream-girl of a romantic imagination. She transcends this not merely through the quality of Marilyn Monroe's performance but because of the effect she has on the other characters. She is to them at one and the same time an attraction and a distraction, a disturbing, disruptive force as well as a soothing, regenerative one. If we are always conscious of her vibrant sexuality, we are never allowed to forget her limitations, though we are not encouraged to maximise them. That she persuades the men, at the end, to release the mustangs they have caught constitutes another change from the ending of the original; that in so doing she seems to be restoring the men's liberty as much as the horses' gives the ending a note of hope hitherto unparalleled in Miller, and this, of course, is intensified by the film's final suggestion of a lasting relationship between Roslyn and Gay.

(3)

The Misfits seemed to belie the common criticism of Miller's work epitomised by Henry Popkin: 'On the whole, Miller's implicit indictment of sex as a wicked influence is remarkably consistent and emphatic'. This is misleading in some respects, for it does not apply at all to *The Man Who Had All the Luck* nor to *All My Sons*. What is criticised in Miller's plays is sex in its anti-family and anti-social manifestations. Willy's sordid liaison with the woman in Boston, Hap's seduction of the executives' fiancées, John Proctor's adultery with Abigail, Eddie Carbone's incestuous promptings towards Catherine — all these are destructive manifestations of sex as an undisciplined passion menacing alike the integrity of the man and the solidarity of the family. Against these must be set, in the same plays, not only the love of Catherine and Rodolpho, but also the confidence in marriage as a satisfactory partnership when both partners are prepared to make it so. This social concern may inhibit a more ecstatically romantic attitude to love, but sex is never so consistently and emphatically wicked an influence in Miller's plays as it is in Tennessee Williams's. It is never the consuming fire that it is in Williams's works, but neither is it the same totally corrupting influence. Willy's extra-marital adventures do not liberate him, but they do not corrupt him either; and if Biff is destroyed in the process, it is by the discovery of his father's imperfection, not directly by sex. The implicit condemnation of the Boston stocking-party is as a betrayal of Linda and Biff, not of Willy.

Far from being 'a wicked influence', sex in *The Misfits* and in other stories of this period is positive and life-giving. Roslyn's persuading of the men to free the horses is not mere soft-heartedness. It is anticipated by her attempt to stop Gay beating the dog and by her distress when he proposes shooting the rabbit that has nibbled the lettuces: 'Couldn't we wait another day and see? I can't stand to kill anything, Gay . . . it's alive and . . . it doesn't know any better, does it?' In the short story 'Please Don't Kill Anything' (1960), a girl urges her sea-shore companion to throw back into the sea some stranded fish: the man tries to force her, for her own good, 'to come to terms with this kind of waste' (like David Beeves and his mink), even demonstrating that the fish eat other fish, 'The victims make other victims'. She persists, and the man laughingly gratifies her whim. What may sound in summary like a piece of flabbily humanitarian sentimentality is given depth by the combination of the girl's innocence, wonder, and capricious feminity with an element of quiet comedy that is relatively new in Miller's work. Miller himself said of *The Misfits* :

There is a change. For a long time now I've wanted to make something of existence. It's tragic — after all, we all die here — but

85

there's something in between. Gay and Roslyn will die, but they can face it with dignity. They can do right and not be like the jerks. It may not sound much but it's taken a lot to get me to that point.[35]

Roslyn's dramatic antecedents are to be found, not in any of his female characters, but in his description of Stockmann in *An Enemy of the People*: 'He might be called the eternal amateur — a lover of things, of people, of sheer living, a man for whom the days are too short, and the future fabulous with discoverable joys . . . He will not compromise for less than God's share of the world'. Trying to sum up these qualities in her, Gay stammers 'You just shine in my eyes . . . I think you're the saddest girl I ever met', but 'You can make a man *feel* happy'. At the end of the film, when Roslyn has conquered her own fears and fought Gay into an acceptance of her values and her belief in life, he tells her 'I never bothered to battle a woman before. And it was peaceful, but a lot like huggin' the air. This time I thought I'd lay my hand on the air again — but it feels like I touched the whole world. I bless you, girl'.

W. J. Weatherby, describing the making of the film on location in Nevada, indicates that Miller changed his mind several times as to how it was to end[36] : was Roslyn to go off with Gay or with Perce? Montgomery Clift, who played Perce, considered that 'Arthur's got it wrong' and was 'doing some wish-fulfilment. He identified with the character played by Gable. Arthur wanted him to keep Marilyn because he wants to himself'. There is, however, in the film itself an internal logic for Miller's ending: Perce is still essentially footloose and Roslyn's inherent insecurity leads her not unnaturally to the older man. To the extent that *The Misfits,* in John Huston's phrase, 'deals with people who will sell their work but not their lives', Miller's theme is still personal integrity, but it is seen now in a happier, less tragic, light.

Despite the sympathy and skill with which Huston directed the film, concentrating on the characters, using black-and-white rather than the distractions of colour, and with a painter's sense of composition, so that Weatherby likens its effects to an etching, it was not an unqualified success either with the critics or at the box-office. Miller had devoted three years to studying the cowboys and the west in his search for authenticity. In its tone, theme, and form of publication, *The Misfits* broke new ground for Miller. Introducing the text of the expanded version he explained that it 'is written in an unfamiliar form, neither novel, play nor screenplay . . . It is a story conceived as a film' and it was 'to create through words the emotions which the finished film should possess'. Describing it as 'a mixed form, if you will, but one which it seems to me has vigorous possibilities for reflecting contemporary existence', he pays tribute to the influence of the cinema on the other creative arts: 'The Misfits avowedly uses the perspectives of the film in order to create a fiction which might have the peculiar immediacy of image and the reflective possibilities of the written word'. He had also been involved in the writing of the script for the 1960 film Let's Make Love, in which Marilyn Monroe and Yves Montand had been directed by George Cukor: was the cinema to influence his future work more than the conventional theatre?

(4)

In 1959 Miller's method of writing had been described by his friend Alan Seager in 'The Creative Agony of Arthur Miller', an essay published in Esquire and quickly reprinted by the English popular magazine Lilliput. According to Seager, Miller begins by filling notebooks with 'aphorisms, scraps of dialogue invented or recalled, short or long poems left incomplete, drawings of sets for as-yet-unconceived plays, personal memoranda in which he talks to himself or asks himself the meaning of some dream or childhood incident, spurts of plotting which may suddenly reveal a whole act, or with luck, the beginning, middle and end of a play'. Seager quotes such pieces of self-advice as 'Beware following the details to the loss of vision', followed by 'Beware following the vision to the loss of details'. Vision in both senses of the word is central to Miller's creativity: when it has been brought satisfactorily into focus there comes the moment when in his own words, 'thinking is left behind. Everything is in the present tense and a play emerges which has resemblances but little else to the mass of notes left behind'.

Detail and vision are not always easy to bring into focus when the playwright's subject is himself: 'personal memoranda' and asking himself 'the meaning of some dream or childhood incident' have in notebooks a legitimate role that may prove intractable in drama. Up to 1960 the autobiographical element in Miller's plays had usually been adequately objectified. A

View from the Bridge would hardly seem to derive very much from Miller's own experience, yet he said he re-wrote it because the first version 'was expressing a very personal preoccupation' and constituted a distant analogy to his own private life. The exact nature of this analogy he leaves unexplained and it may be indiscernible to the outsider, none of whose business, strictly speaking, it is. It may, of course, be the problem of ethnicity which had preoccupied him earlier in *Focus* and in the delicately-handled short story 'Monte Sant' Angelo' (1951). If, in the play, it is obliquely approached through Eddie's Sicilian heritage, the subsequent emphasis on the wider implications of the social play and the *polis* may be intended to divert attention from it.

Alternatively, Eddie's smotheringly protective love for his young niece may have seemed to Miller an uncomfortable parallel to his own relations with Marilyn Monroe. Montgomery Clift, objecting to Roslyn going off with Gay, puts it thus :

> When Marilyn first went to Hollywood, Gable was a father figure to her. It's like a girl going with her father. No, Arthur's got it wrong. Maybe that's what's wrong with his relationship with her. Maybe he was too paternal. I know she respected him too much, looked up to him. All idols fall eventually.

Miller's vacillation over the ending must have been affected by the realisation that, while filming was in progress, the marriage was disintegrating. Marilyn told Weatherby later :

> When we were first married, he saw me as so beautiful and innocent among the Hollywood wolves that I tried to be like that . . . But when the monster showed, Arthur couldn't believe it. I disappointed him when that happened . . . I put Arthur through a lot, I know. But he also put me through a lot. It's never one-sided.

Disillusion, divorce and Marilyn's suicide must inevitably have raised acutely for Miller problems of personal responsibility over which a book of this nature could normally have drawn a veil. For one whose plays have always been rooted in guilt, however, the impulse to explore these issues dramatically was equally inevitable; Weatherby believes that Miller's third wife, Inge Morath, encouraged him to exorcise on stage this and other ghosts from the past at which the earlier plays had only hinted. Re-marriage brought its consolations, but the confident belief, when he was writing *The Misfits,* that he could 'make something of existence' would not be quickly regained. His interest in the cinema seemed also to have been dissipated, and he returned to the theatre with a play which, though superficially innovatory, is as retrospective in form as in subject matter. Even to his admirers it was a disappointment.

7

After the Fall

(1)

'The Inside of his Head' would have made a better alternative title for *After the Fall* than for *Death of a Salesman*. The dramatic form Miller evolved for the later play is dictated by this concept and suggests how *Death of a Salesman* might have been constructed had Miller believed the theatre in 1949 (or even perhaps himself as a playwright) to have been ready for it. More fluid than its predecessor, its easier fluctuations in time, place and mood enable it to take on more issues and more widely-ranging ones, public as well as private. The fifteen years between the two plays had enriched Miller's experience and his skill as a dramatist; most of the themes in *After the Fall* had preoccupied him in earlier works and seemed now to be brought together for a mature re-examination of their interacting complexities.

For all its apparent adventurousness, however, the fluidity of form works against it. The scenes of recall in *Death of a Salesman,* involving as they do a change of acting area, sometimes changes of costume, sometimes the introduction of a few properties, acquire the status of inset episodes; they have a duration and an identity that make a sharper theatrical impact than the more fragmented, kaleidoscopic glimpses of the past in *After the Fall*. The demonstrable sequence in which they recur, being dictated by Willy's sub-conscious, determines more clearly the structure and thrust of the play, affording an ordered and progressive disclosure of his personal guilt and respon-sibility for what has happened. This, together with the sense of an on-going dramatic action not yet concluded, sustains the element of surprise and thus the audience's interest.

The form of *After the Fall* is essentially the dramatic monologue interspersed by representations of past events, and in the theatre this is no real substitute for dramatic action. That Quentin is on stage throughout, speaking directly to the audience, might seem to place him more fully in control than Willy of the re-presentation of the past but in fact it emphasises the static nature of the play. In the cinema 'voice-over' techniques could keep Quentin-in-the-present in the audience's mind's eye less obtrusively; on stage he is too literally in their vision. This and the fact that he has already accepted, more fully and more consciously than Willy, the extent of his personal guilt for the past, puts the play at the disadvantage of seeming only to re-hash a sequence of events already concluded. Dramatic *tour de force* that the role of Quentin indisputably is, it nevertheless imposes on the character a passivity and a completeness that Willy, though the lesser man, does not have in the theatre.

A 'stream of consciousness' play in a sense that *Death of a Salesman* is not, *After the Fall* relies, with greater sophistication, on an associational process of recall more real in its seeming inconsequentiality than Willy's. Psychologically it is thus less 'artificial' but, *pace* much modern experimentation, the theatre itself *is* artificial and plays *are* artifacts. Acceptance of this does not force all drama into outworn and stereotyped moulds, but it may help to concentrate the playwright's mind on what is feasible and effective on the stage.

One critic in 1965 saw this new play as a failure because it 'remains a realistic play with scenes rearranged in time and space'. It is more genuinely experimental than that, but what he calls 'Miller's unquenchable devotion to realism' seems to me to create one problem. To suggest a world external to his characters Miller uses non-speaking extras who pass across the stage or materialise in momentary tableaux. There are more than two dozen of these, together with three or four characters who, though named, have only one line or so to deliver. Not only is this uneconomical but it may too easily confuse the audience, who will inevitably expect some at least of these walking-on characters to make a larger contribution to the continuing story-line than in fact they do. It may also be questioned whether such background figures would really feature in Quentin's stream of consciousness and thus whether their introduction is not superfluous and the result of a mixture of methods.

This play was, of course, commissioned as the opening production at the new Lincoln Center for the Performing Arts in New York City. Such occasions encourage the display of the theatre's flexibility and adaptability in ways to which the conventional proscenium-arch, 'fourth-wall-removed' kind of play lends itself less readily, and at least one critic commended the original production for moving 'like mist over the platforms and parapets of the big, open acting area . . . There is no picture-frame stage, no curtain, no scenery, no teasers to hide lights. It is a theater of revealment for a drama of revealment'. The sets were designed by Jo Mielziner who had designed the original *Death of a Salesman;* Elia Kazan, who had directed that play but not worked with Miller since, directed *After the Fall*.

The play has grandness of conception and boldness of design: the role of Quentin is a virtuoso piece of writing which produced a widely-acclaimed performance from Jason Robards. *The Saturday Evening Post* announced enthusiastically that 'he joins in active dialogue for three solid hours, an even longer role than Hamlet's'. Others, however, were quick to condemn the scale of the play as reflecting self-indulgence on the author's part rather than artistic greatness.

(2)

The *Post's* comment accompanied its publication of the complete text of this 'powerful drama' within a week of the opening which it hailed as a 'national experience'. In a specially-written foreword Miller dwelt characteristically on the large moral implications of a play that he defined as 'the trial of a man by his own conscience, his own values, his own deeds'. Admittedly the cover featured Barbara Loden, the actress who created the role of Maggie, as a 'sensational new find' and referred to Miller's 'hottest new play since *Death of a Salesman'*, but in no other respect did the *Post's* presentation impute to the play any sensationalism.

Three weeks later *Life International* announced on its cover: 'Marilyn's Ghost. Arthur Miller writes about his shocking new play'. Inside, Tom Prideaux, after the tribute (already quoted) to 'a drama of revealment', asked pointedly whether too much was revealed and decided that 'Quentin protests too much' in the 'kind of moral strip-tease' that he performs, especially in the first half of the play. 'The second half', he declared 'takes fire as it focuses sharply on Maggie.' Identifying her with Marilyn Monroe, he exonerated Miller from the charge of 'serious bad taste' that was being brought against him, and praised instead his courage in telling 'the truth, as he saw it, against himself'.

Miller's own one-page article which followed was entitled 'With respect for her agony — but with love'. It expressed surprise at the outcry, which he saw as hypocritical, of people who charged him with 'cruelty toward the memory of Marilyn Monroe' and denied that Maggie is a representation of Marilyn: she is only 'a character in a play about the human animal's unwillingness or inability to discover in himself the seeds of his own destruction'. Again he shifts the argument, with dignity as well as deftness, on to a higher and wider moral plane, but he does it much more defensively than in the rather Olympian foreword in the *Post*. The debate that was to bedevil so much discussion of this play had begun. As Prideaux observed, however much Miller repeated that Maggie was not the real Marilyn, 'the play itself invites the comparison — not invites, insists on, really'. W.J. Weatherby points out that not only was Barbara Loden made to look as much like Marilyn as possible, but at least one incident is taken straight from Marilyn's life: 'she had had an affair with a leading Hollywood agent who was married and whose family excluded her when he died even though his last words were about her'.[37] That, in Maggie's account of this, the agent should have been transformed into a judge requires some modification of my earlier comments on the high esteem in which Miller usually holds lawyers, but it does not diminish the significance of his inclusion of the incident.[38] As Weatherby says, 'There are too many incidents and remarks that recall the Miller-Monroe relationship for the play not to seem a revelation of what went on behind the scenes and to be Miller's view of what went wrong . . . But many admirers of hers were indignant at the portrait and the interpretation'. All in all, it was obviously ingenuous of Miller to express the hope that, within the foreseeable future, the play can be separated from 'Marilyn's golden image'.

What was largely at issue, of course, was the tarnishing of that image. The golden girl of *The Misfits*, whose insecurity had ripened into love, had been supplanted by this drug-addicted neurotic whose insecurity had extinguished love, and in whom the fey, trusting innocence of Roslyn had given way to moral irresponsibility, egotistic and unfeeling arrogance, and a vulgar viciousness. Weatherby speaks of Maggie as 'the other side of

Roslyn . . . the missing side that made her unsatisfying in the movie and hard for Monroe to make convincing', but to many people it looked as though, in Maggie, Miller had portrayed too emphatically the 'monster' that Marilyn had accused him of being unable to accept in her. People do not take kindly to the destruction of their myths, nor, indeed to the insistence that they *are* myths. Here, in their indignation, they blamed Miller for the destruction of something when he was in reality trying to show them that, if it had ever existed at all, it had in fact destroyed itself. Quentin/Miller is agonising over his own inability to arrest that process, and even questioning whether it was not, perhaps, unwillingness as much as inability; this however, moved the audience less (understandably) than the recentness of the painful events he was dramatising. The rawness of Maggie/Marilyn's agony was more apparent to them than the respect and love which Miller claimed had prompted him to the depiction of it. The relationship between Quentin and Maggie culminates with dramatic appropriateness in this realisation: 'Maggie, we were both born of many errors; a human being has to forgive himself! Neither of us is innocent. What more do you want?' [p.116]. Fearful that he himself cannot love, he tries to force from her the admission ' "And I am full of hatred; I, Maggie, sweet lover of all life — I hate the world!" ' [p.114]. Looked at dispassionately this says, about their respective responsibilities for the break-up, little more than Marilyn Monroe had already admitted privately to W.J. Weatherby. Reviewing the opening performance in *The New York Times* as 'a pain-wracked drama . . . Mr. Miller's maturest', Howard Taubman rightly insisted that 'it seeks to understand, not to judge'. Accepting this, many people still felt uncomfortably voyeuristic at being involved in the process, and their inability successfully to disengage Maggie from Marilyn (especially when Barbara Loden's appearance so strongly resembled that of the dead star) should not have surprised Miller as totally as it seems to have done.

(3)

Yet even if the passage of time has blunted sensibilities on this score, the structure of *After the Fall* still confronts us with critical problems. So compelling in its intensity is the treatment of Maggie that, as Tom Prideaux pointed out, the second part of the play does indeed take fire in its concentration on that theme. The first part by contrast, is less clear in its thrust, more uneasy in its movement. Before it has opened the Maggie theme, the first part has tried to encompass Quentin's relationship with his parents and brother, his first wife Louise, two mistresses (Felice and Elsie), as well as his friends Lou (Elsie's husband) and Mickey, with whom he shares a past involvement in left-wing politics; it also introduces his developing relationship with the German girl Holga and his sense of involvement, through her, in the anti-Semitism of the Nazi concentration camps.

It is questionable whether the fragmented episodic stream-of-consciousness method is really adequate in the establishment of so many and such varied themes. Are *both* Felice and Elsie essential? Is the political theme sufficiently developed? That Lou's suicide should relieve Quentin of the necessity for a painful moral decision is, like Maggie's suicide, in line with the play's recurrent suggestion that Quentin is in some ways the man who had all the luck — his problems are removed before he has to solve them — but the guilt is the more oppressive because of that. Nevertheless, Lou's suicide tends to look more like a trick of dramatic convenience, and Mickey's disappearance from the play unfortunately reinforces this impression. What is no doubt a conscientious attempt to keep this one theme in proportion to the others begins to look unfortunately like an evasion of it. By making Quentin a lawyer by profession Miller may intend a secularisation of the Catholic adage *corruptio optimi est pessima*[39] : that the wisdom, firmness of judgement, and moral rightness associated with that profession in the earlier plays are not evident here could constitute a significant indictment of the perturbed times, but although Quentin agonises over Lou and Mickey he never seems as professionally involved with the issue as one would have expected Miller to make him.

Moreover, to counterpoint Quentin's lack of involvement there with his growing interest in Maggie is unfortunately to belittle both. Quentin forgets to attend the meeting of his colleagues specially convened to discuss his and the firm's future if he persists in the defence of Lou; his forgetfulness is occasioned, in the action of the play, by his first chance meeting with Maggie in the park, and is subsequently rationalised by

95

Louise as a manifestation of unconscious fear. Yet neither of these, nor even the combination of them, carries quite enough credibility. What sort of a lawyer, already divided between loyalty to a friend and professional self-interest, allows the issue to be driven so casually out of his mind? Whatever fascination Maggie exudes, and however emotionally upset Quentin already is, could such an infatuation take him so quickly and so completely 'out of this world'?

His dilemma over whether or not to defend Lou is at once complicated and simplified by two other elements that merit closer scrutiny than Miller allows him to give them. One is Lou's admission that, in the original book on the revision of which he is now working, he had deliberately suppressed evidence unfavourable to the Communist cause. Of course, as the play is concerned with Quentin's discovery that no one can be as innocent as he has believed them to be, some imperfection in Lou has to be demonstrated. However, Lou's fear of 'being forced to defend my own incredible lies' leaves ambiguous the extent to which the new book will actually repudiate the old; Mickey attributes the lies in the earlier version to Elsie's influence more than to Lou's dedication to the cause; and Elsie's impassioned hostility to the publication of the new book may be ascribed to any of several causes unspecified in the text. Quentin's readiness to judge others is reiterated by several characters in the play, including himself, yet on all these issues he takes no steps to satisfy himself and passes no explicit judgment. Psychologically explicable as this may be, dramatically it requires more clarification than Miller gives it. The reluctance to pose the matter in terms too sharply black and white is characteristic of him and commendable, but it leads to an obfuscation difficult to penetrate in print and almost impossible in the theatre. That Lou's wife, Elsie, is yet another woman to whom Quentin is sexually attracted is again consistent with Quentin's extra-marital adventurousness, but its implications for Quentin's attitude to the defence of Lou are insufficiently explored. It is for reasons such as these that Lou's suicide seems contrived to let Miller off the dramatic hook as much as to let Quentin off the moral one.

More strikingly, however, than any other of his plays, *After the Fall* polarises differences of critical response, and at least one commentator describes the first half of the play as 'a

The Misfits: Arthur Miller (in glasses), John Huston (standing, in hat) and (front, left to right) Montgomery Clift, Marilyn Monroe and Clark Gable (1961)

The Misfits: Marilyn Monroe (*Roslyn*), Clark Gable (*Gay*)

towering achievement':

> The form unfolds as the mind touches various events revealing decisive details of Quentin's life and asking the audience to be concerned with the limits of love, the response of the beloved, the meaning of friendship, justice, truth. Miller imposes no specific dogma, but asks for common speculation into mutual concerns.

This assumes that the play will necessarily stimulate the concern for which it asks, and, like the play itself, it assumes concern to be an adequate form of audience-involvement. Harsh as it is to say so, Quentin is concerned with all these issues, and he has feelings about them that do him credit; for a lawyer, he may seem to many laymen to be guided far too quickly by his emotions and his concern, far too little by the intellect on which his professional success has presumably depended. The theatre is not a debating chamber, but the audience's concern might be more readily engaged and developed into a constructive interest if Quentin's concern were more convincingly seen to be the rational product of self-analysis and a growing understanding of his predicament.

The associated themes of Holga and the concentration camps also seem to me posited rather than developed and integrated with the rest. We need to be sure that Holga is not merely the latest in the succession of women in whom Quentin has pinned his faith, and that the experiences he has undergone really have developed in Quentin a capacity for love. These things are implied but are they established? Is it an economy of dramatic method or a cutting of dramatic corners?

The play begins and ends with Quentin saying 'Hello!' The first 'Hello!' is a natural, unobtrusive greeting of the unseen interlocutor represented by the audience; the final 'Hello!' is in reply to Holga's and the exchange is clearly intended to signal a new beginning, as does his upward movement towards her through the ranks of the other characters with whom he has presumably come finally to terms. (If the final stage-direction reference to them as 'endlessly alive' is intended in any way to qualify this impression it is hard to see how it could be realised on the stage.) The significance of the 'Hello!' is underlined further by the division between the two acts. The first act ends, apart from a two-line exchange between Quentin and Maggie, with Quentin telling the 'listener': 'I'd like to settle this. Although actually I (*laughs*) only came to say hello'; the second opens with Holga greeting him warmly 'Quentin! Here! Hello!' Hello!'

A similar underlining is effected by another recurrent phrase. At the end of Quentin's long opening speech after the initial 'Hello!' he tells the 'listener': '. . . the truth is that every morning when I awake, I'm full of hope! . . . I open my eyes, I'm like a boy!'. At the end of the act he repeats it: 'I open up my eyes each morning like a boy, even now'. At the end of the play Holga 'materialises' for the last time, repeating her phrase 'But no one is innocent they did not kill!' and then bidding him 'Hello!'; Quentin responds to her hope by reiterating 'And that, that's why I wake each morning like a boy — even now, even now! I swear to you, I could love the world again!'. The process by which the regained faith is conveyed to us is discernible and effective; the process by which it has been achieved would have been clearer if the action had allowed a fuller development of Holga as a character and not merely an inspiration. This in turn might have made the concentration camp theme something more than the rather facile symbol of a wider guilt that it sometimes seems.

(4)

These strictures are in no way intended to impugn Miller's sincerity and depth of feeling nor to minimise the reality of the psychological and moral insights he has brought to it. What the play says is both pertinent and admirable, but in the theatre are its themes of guilt and moral responsibility sufficiently articulated dramatically as distinct from verbally? However acceptable its 'philosophy' may be, it must be conveyed by the play as a whole and not merely by homiletic speeches. That 'The action takes place in the mind, thought, and memory of Quentin' does not exonerate the playwright from the duty of providing a dramatic action that is seen to have a unity in the Aristotelian and not merely the psychologically-subjective sense.

For Quentin as for Willy Loman, images arise from the family past to torment him. Two of these revive the 'two brothers' pattern: the simpler is the memory of the childhood incident when the parents took his elder brother Dan to Atlantic City, sending Quentin for a walk with the maid to avoid having to take him too. The toy sailing boat they bring him back is no compensation for the sense of betrayal which, he later decides, is 'the only truth that sticks'. It seems to have been one of the rare occasions when he did not get what he wanted, for the second memory is of his having been given the opportunity of a college education by Dan's self-sacrifice in staying at home to support their father. Quentin's guilt at this surfaces in the play when he recalls his father's reproach:'What you *want!* Always what you *want!* Chris-sake, *what are you!'* [p.89].

These incidents, together with Quentin's third and most haunting memory of his father's ruin in the Depression of the 1930s, are grafted neatly into the action of *After the Fall,* most of them in Act II. The sailboat memory first occurs, with appropriate irony, when he accuses himself of trying to love everybody: it reminds him of his inability to mourn his mother and modulates into his inability to mourn Maggie. The college memory occurs when Holga's fear that 'I may not be all that interesting' is contrasted with Louise's assertion 'I am not all this uninteresting, Quentin!': he contemplates leaving Holga as he has left Louise ('there *is* some freedom in the going') only to recall how his mother, who idolised him as a child, encouraged him in what he now sees as the treason of deserting his father in order to pursue his own ambition. Dan's promise to 'send you a list of books to read' dissolves neatly into another time as Maggie immediately asks in reply, 'But could I read them?'.

The most traumatic of these experiences is introduced even more skilfully at a much earlier stage of the play and is developed into a more extended scene [pp.25-30]. Triggered off by his visit with Holga to the concentration camp, it comes so unexpectedly as to force from him the question 'But what the hell has this got to do with a concentration camp?'. To some extent he has anticipated this in his previous speech, when he recognises his inability to weep as Holga can at 'this slaughter-house' with which he feels an understanding, and when he links this with his inability to mourn his mother. (The only 'family recall' scene to precede this has been of breaking to his father the news of the mother's death and realising that he himself does not 'seem to know how to grieve for her'.) The scene begins deceptively on a note of comedy: Quentin as a child is being smartened up to attend his uncle's wedding, and his mother's meandering monologue ranges over the inadequacies of his handwriting, speech and posture, her brother's capacity to make every wedding in the family a catastrophe, and her husband's absence from the last such occasion through falling asleep in a Turkish bath. Pride in her husband's personality clashes with memories of his earlier illiteracy and of the college career she sacrificed to marry him; at the same time she recalls sentimentally the penniless medical student her father had injudiciously forbidden her to marry ('Who knew he'd end up so big in the gallstones?' she asks rhetorically). This promising vein of Jewish humour is exploited further when her husband assures her he has not forgotten the wedding: 'I wish I could, but I'm paying for it . . . They all fall in love on my money. I married into a love nest!' Then, with appalling suddenness, it is sabotaged by the phone conversation to which, uncomprehendingly, she listens as he discovers that he is bankrupt. The cross-examination by which she establishes the full extent of the disaster rises from incredulity to vituperation and contemptuous abuse culminating in a final estranging insult 'You are an idiot!'

A beautifully managed, though painful, scene in its own right, it also exhibits Miller's stagecraft by its dramatic release of what is to be a key word throughout the play. In vain does the mother, a moment later, deny to Quentin that she has insulted his father ('Well, I was a little angry, that's all, but I never said *that*. I think he's a wonderful man!'): she compounds the cruelty by the well-meant deceit, and the treachery is unforgettable. At crisis after crisis Quentin will remember his mother uttering the one word 'Idiot!' Yet the fact that the word, or a derivative of it, occurs at least fourteen times in the play and is only on four of these associated specifically with his mother's use of it illustrates the firmness with which Miller implants it in our consciousness and the effectiveness with which he draws on the association. Elsie's reiterated 'He's a moral idiot!' is deliberately ambiguous in its application: she may mean Mickey, she may mean her husband, she may even mean Quentin, and since Quentin remembering her use of the phrase always remembers her drawing her bathrobe across her as she says it, he obviously regards it as an exclusion of him from the intimacy that the falling open of her robe has first occasioned between them.

One powerful recurrence of the word shows how deeply it has

seared into Quentin's mind. It occurs when he is desperately trying to force Maggie into an admission of her own responsibility for what is happening to them. 'If you could only say', he tells her, ' "I have been cruel", this frightening room would open. If you could say, "I have been kicked around, but I have been just as inexcusably vicious to others, called my husband idiot in public . . ." ' [pp.113-114]. Now on the evidence of the text, this is something that Maggie has *not* done. Louise has, but only in private, Elsie may have, but Maggie has not. Yet to Quentin, convinced as he is of Maggie's turpitude, it is inconceivable that she should not have been guilty, like his mother, of this peculiarly heinous act of treachery. Even in this 'drama of revealment' this instinctive transfer of the mother's guilt to the wife is outstanding as a revelation of Quentin's state of mental distress: it is a masterly touch but it may be too subtle to make in the theatre the full impact that it should.

Counterpointing this savage melody of 'idiot', however, is another, more tender one that is introduced almost as soon as the original clash between Quentin's parents has dissolved back to the concentration camp. Holga, whose hopefulness Quentin admires, tells him 'I think it's a mistake to ever look for hope outside one's self' and goes on to describe a recurring dream that she has experienced :

> I dreamed I had a child, and even in the dream I saw it was my life, and it was an idiot, and I ran away. But it always crept on to my lap again, clutched at my clothes. Until I thought, if I could kiss it, whatever in it was my own, perhaps I could sleep. And I bent to its broken face, and it was horrible . . . but I kissed it. I think one must finally take one's life in one's arms, Quentin. [pp.30-31].

Parabolically it embodies the 'message' of the play, perhaps a little too sententiously, but there is real skill in this linking of the two themes: acceptance of the idiot child exorcises the 'Idiot!' The play has some way to go before Quentin learns this lesson, but the 'idiot child' image haunts him, and Quentin, when he does something that he regrets, almost always speaks of it as 'idiotic', thus ambivalently evoking both motifs.

(5)

By another dextrous piece of counterpointing Quentin's response to this speech of Holga's releases a word that is a

101

useful key to another of the play's main themes. Fumblingly, all he can say is, 'It sounds foolish, but I feel . . . unblessed'. As he does so, he momentarily visualises Felice as a reminder to himself and to the audience that in one respect he is embarrassed to be as blessed as he is. 'I'll always bless you. Always!', Felice has told him on her first appearance, and this time too, though she does not speak, she 'holds up her hand in blessing'. Whenever she is recalled it is in association with this single act. At the very end of the play Felice is again automatically about to raise her arm in blessing when 'he shakes her hand, aborting her enslavement'. There is an ambiguity here: is it her enslavement of him by her perpetual benediction that is being aborted, or is he freeing her from her enslavement *to* him? In the theatre the distinction is unimportant: the silent gesture merely terminates a relationship. The stage direction has, however, implications that merit discussion, for either interpretation or both can be supported from the text. Quentin has already admitted to us 'There's something about that girl unnerves me . . . And she meant so little to me. I feel like a mirror in which she saw herself as glorious'. Yet the memory of her recurs time and again, enslaving him to the guilt it evokes. The confidence and the self-respect Felice has derived from her relationship with him are, of course, precisely what he gives initially to Maggie. Inevitably the two are later recalled in this context simultaneously and Quentin recognises that 'there is a fraud involved; I have no such power'. Felice's attitude remains constant and he cannot bear it: 'It frightens me, and I wish to God she'd stop blessing me!' [p.72].

Felice's sole function in the play is thus to epitomise for us Quentin's capacity to inspire in others a confidence and a love that he is unable adequately to reciprocate. She, alone of his four 'pre-Holga' women, sustains her love for him despite this and can always bless him: perhaps because of this she is dramatically the least realised of all of them. The phrase that she uses to convey her affection has other resonances, though. '"I bless you, girl",' Gay told Roslyn, and it is the nearest Miller allows himself to go in implying a happy ending to *The Misfits*. 'I bless you, Quentin!' says Maggie in the second act of this play, and it is linked in his memory with his mother blessing him earlier. 'God bless this child', says the black servant Carrie at Maggie's wedding: it is the only specific mention of God in conjunction with what is elsewhere consistently an expression of affection. 'I bless you' may well be another of those phrases of Miller's that has a Jewish origin, but its force in this play is unmistakeable. The nearest Quentin comes to it is significant: "Holga, I bless your uncertainty. You don't seem to be looking for some goddamned . . . moral *victory*'. [p.24]. By the end of the play such victory as he has achieved may seem singularly Pyrrhic, but what he has learnt could, not inappropriately, be formulated in W.H. Auden's lines, 'And life remains a blessing / Although you cannot bless'.

Quentin's final speech, expressing tentatively such conclusions as he has reached, is, in its hesitant eloquence, as fine as any Miller has written. It brings together the dominant themes of the play melodically in a *reprise* of the key phrases and ideas :

> What burning cities taught her and the death of love taught me . . . that's why I woke each morning like a boy . . . To know, and even happily, that we meet unblessed . . . after the Fall . . . Is the knowing all? And the wish to kill is never killed, but with some gift of courage one may look into its face when it appears, and with a stroke of love — as to an idiot in the house — forgive it . . . [p.120].

The most humane of all Miller's plays up to this point, *After the Fall* is ultimately concerned with forgiveness, but not in a sentimental way. Ironically, had it been more sentimental, less candid in its analysis of Maggie, it would have occasioned less hostility and been more readily judged on dramatic than on moral grounds. It would still not have been one of his best plays in the theatre: it lacks *The Crucible's* simple directness of dramatic line and *Death of a Salesman's* newness of dramatic idiom; the dilemma of its protagonist is more specialised and personal. Yet, like all of Miller's plays, it is a gloss on the idea expressed by Meredith :

> In tragic life, God wot,
No villain need be; passion spins the plot:
We are betrayed by what is false within.

Quietly but firmly, however, it denies the possibility of apportioning the blame to outside forces that is still as available to Willy Loman's sympathisers as it was to Willy.

After the Fall, for all its faults, merits respect greater than is sometimes accorded it and closer critical attention than is possible in the theatre. Its text can reveal to the student a carefully-patterned structure and an integrity of approach to which, in the future, when the rawness of feeling about Marilyn Monroe has tempered more with the passing of time, a revival may be able to do more justice on the stage.

8

Incident at Vichy

(1)

Also written for the Lincoln Center, *Incident at Vichy* appeared in the same year as *After the Fall* and was hailed in *The New York Times* by Howard Taubman as 'one of the most important plays of our time' with its 'towering moral passion'. Its subject, the persecution of the Jews, had been, in its more localised and less spectacular manifestations, the theme of some of Miller's prose fiction, most notably *Focus*. The strength of Miller's feeling about it is beyond dispute, but neither this nor the importance of its subject makes it necessarily as significant a piece of theatre as Taubman suggests.

In *After the Fall* guilt for the Second World War genocide of the Jews is seen to differ only in degree and not in kind from the more personal guilts that so torment the overburdened Quentin. A particularly revealing comparison occurs in Miller's *Life* magazine defence of that play in the face of the attacks on it :

> The whole business reminds me of the righteous indignation which greeted Hannah Arendt's controversial book, *Eichmann in Jerusalem*. It seemed to me, reading it, that she was trying to make a spectacularly simple and quite evident point. Namely, that the significant truth about Eichmann was not that he was a monster but that, in order to exercise his monstrousness — to be in a position to murder — he had to have the moral permission of others. In trying to prove her thesis, the author extended that permissiveness even to Jews and to well-meaning Gentiles who, despite all, were less than total in their active opposition to barbarity. But the suggestion that 'we' could, in even a remote way, bear responsibility for what 'we' abhor was turned upside down by some people so that Miss Arendt was made to seem an apologist for Eichmann.

Incident at Vichy is, of course, a dramatisation of precisely that view, the monstrousness of the perpetrators being in some ways less terrifying than the acquiescence of the well-meaning.

In the same article he had claimed that 'Maggie most perfectly exemplifies the self-destructiveness which finally comes when one views oneself as pure victim': the idea had received an earlier and less expected formulation in 'Please Don't Kill Anything' when the fishes prompt the moral 'The victims make other victims'. Out of the coalescence in his creative imagination of these and other ideas Miller fashions *Incident at Vichy* but, stimulating and provocative as they are, the play fails to do them full justice. For one thing, its one-act brevity is hardly proportionate to their complex gravity. It is as though, having heeded the complaints that *After the Fall* was too long and too ponderous, he had over-compensated here by compression but without altogether eliminating the ponderousness.

There is also a detached coldness about the dramatisation that is in one sense paradoxically to his credit. That a man so conscious of his own Jewish heritage and preoccupied over so many years with the problems of ethnic minorities in the modern world should tackle so inflammatory a subject as Nazi extermination policies would seem an invitation to melodrama. Again, he may be over-compensating for the alleged self-indulgence of *After the Fall*, or it may be that the intensity of his feelings on the subject alerts him to the necessity for a tightness of dramatic control and a concentration on moral abstractions rather than on physical suffering.

The plot may be summarised briefly and with minimal prejudice to the enjoyment of the play in performance. In Vichy in 1942 a random group of suspects awaits interrogation by the Germans to determine whether they are Jews. The interrogation takes place off-stage; some return to be released, others are not seen again. Eventually two remain: one is given a release-permit which he passes to the other who is certain of condemnation. With his escape the play ends. Ungrateful as the criticism sounds, the whole subject is handled too dispassionately, too responsibly, and in too low a key for success in the theatre.

(2)

Again Miller uses too many characters. A cast of twenty-one for a one-act play makes differentiation and development of individual characters unnecessarily difficult: Harold Clurman's notes as director of the first production are much preoccupied with this.[40] Each can be shown to contribute something to the whole, but in some cases (the gypsy, for instance) it is too little to matter. Moreover, even when ten or more people are simultaneously on stage, Miller tends to restrict conversation to only two or three at a time, leaving the rest, until eventually they are given a few more lines, with little to do beyond registering despondency and apprehension. So large a cast calls attention to the play's static nature, and this is insufficiently redeemed by the quality of the dialogue.

Here Miller's usual flair seems to have forsaken him. The subject is serious, the situation tense, but the conversation too readily takes on a philosophical gravity that does not quite ring true and laces this with a vocabulary and idiom that are at times too American for the context. This is not to ask for the broken English sometimes supposed indispensable to the stage representation of continental Europeans, but references to clams, pressed pants, S.S. bums and sons-of-bitches jar a little, as does the phrase 'He plays a beautiful piano' used to describe the musician's skill and not the instrument's quality. A more neutrally colloquial speech seems desirable to convey feeling informally but with some intensity. It is not easy, either, to accept that Nazis would discuss the value of circumcision as evidence of Jewishness in quite the polite, formal and oblique manner that these do. Taken singly, these things are trivial: collectively they point to an uncertain control of dialogue unusual in Miller, and there are few of the felicities of phrase or lifts of tone that distinguish the other plays.

With his material, too, Miller does not seem at ease and relies uncharacteristically on coincidence. Leduc, a French doctor, finds himself detained in Vichy in the company of an Austrian prince whose cousin he has met in Vienna previously: this might be acceptable if Leduc did not also turn out to have a prior acquaintance with the German major who is to interrogate them. The brief and singularly limp speech in which he identifies the major bristles with inconsistencies: 'I was in the Sixteenth Artillery, facing you [at Amiens in June 1940]. I recognize your insignia, which of course I could hardly forget' [p.164].[41] If Leduc is a doctor, what was he doing in the army as a combat officer? (He has defined himself as such at p.163.) If he was with the artillery rather than the infantry he is hardly likely to have been close enough to the enemy to identify one man's insignia, and if, by some means, he did, why is the memory so indelible? Surprisingly, this recognition plays no part whatever in the plot, nor is it essential that Leduc should be a doctor. Normally Miller would make so moralistic a figure a lawyer, especially as his medical qualifications are not adduced as a reason why Von Berg should allow him to escape at the end.

Another incident that seems to have little point is Bayard's breaking of the handle off the gypsy's pot and pocketing it. It presumably refers back to his advice to the others that any sharp implement will enable them to chisel away the wood around the freight car door and thus escape from the train that will take them to the concentration camp; however, his early disappearance from the play and the impossibility of developing the handle-breaking incident in any way mean that, if it is noticed at all, it will either puzzle the audience or its full significance will escape them. It is an unusual complaint to make of Miller as a dramatist.

(3)

The play is, however, an object-lesson in the sustaining of tension with minimal action. That Harold Clurman thought of it as 'A medallion or emblem engraved on metal or stone' underlines its static quality. Howard Taubman's enumeration of all its moments of 'fierce action' seems somewhat defensive, as does his assurance that the 'steady attrition of victims is in itself a dramatic device of unfaltering suspense'. The play does generate tension by, for example, the recurrent discussion of whether to rush the guard, even though the expectations thus raised are not fulfilled: so unheroic a group would never attempt an escape, but the audience continues to hope. The passivity, of course, heightens by contrast the sudden impulsiveness of Von Berg's gift of his pass to Leduc and Leduc's escape, with which the play ends.

To call it a worthy piece may sound patronising but it is unavoidable, and indicates the extent to which its merits are more literary than theatrical. Links with other Miller plays are not hard to discern, as when Von Berg says of his title: 'It is not a "title"; it is my name, my family. Just as you have a name and a family. And you are not inclined to dishonour them, I presume' [p.169]. Yet when the Major describes himself as 'a man of honour' but regards the respect and love of others as

108

irrelevant we are in a world where honour is indeed but a word. Yet it is again a play about integrity and has, as one would expect, a thoughtful sincerity, an accuracy of observation, and a humane concern for people. At the same time it does not sentimentalise people. There is a telling moment early in the play when the actor Monceau, unwilling to believe in Nazi atrocities, insists that 'War is war, but you still have to keep a certain sense of proportion. I mean Germans are still *people*'. Bayard can credit the atrocities because 'they're Fascists', but Leduc can believe 'exactly because they are people' [p.168]. Later Von Berg makes a similar point: the atrocity is believable 'Because it *is* so inconceivably vile. That is their power. To do the inconceivable; it paralyses the rest of us' [p.180].

Yet not to make monsters of the Nazis he presents is a tribute to Miller's dramatic tact, as well as to his reading of Hannah Arendt. It is an effective piece of theatre to allow Von Berg, before his attitudes have emerged with any sharpness of definition, to speak of Nazism merely as 'an outburst of vulgarity', to explain dispassionately Nazi resentment towards members of noble families like himself, and to reflect on the inadequacy of taste and art to withstand totalitarianism [pp.170-171]. The main action of the play is the change in Von Berg from the confused, ineffectual aristocrat of this scene to the man who sacrifices himself for Leduc at the end. Convincing but in no way sensational, it typifies the low key of the play.

This is accentuated by Miller's instinctive concentration on the victims rather than the oppressors. That the detainees outnumber their captors and yet are powerless against them reflects the condition of occupied France, but the multiplicity of characters does allow some differentiation between their attitudes to that condition. Here the contrast between Monceau and Leduc is crucial. Both believe in a society ordered by law:

> MONCEAU: I go on the assumption that if I obey the law with dignity I will live in peace. I may not like the law, but evidently the majority does, or they would overthrow it. And I'm speaking now of the French majority, who outnumber the Germans in this town fifty to one. [p.190].

Leduc's entry earlier has been made on a note of rational protest:

109

LEDUC: Sir, I must ask the reason for this. I am a combat officer, captain in the French Army. There is no authority to arrest me in French territory. The Occupation has not revoked French law in southern France. [p.163].

This appeal to the law is dismissed contemptuously in one word: 'Speech-maker', says one of his captors. Nevertheless it is only after Leduc has weighed carefully Bayard's, Lebeau's, and Monceau's impressions of what is going on that he is prepared, in the exchange with Monceau already mentioned, to give credence to the German atrocities.

Monceau, on the other hand, remains unshakeable in his reiterated conviction that some people attract disaster to themselves by adopting too readily the passive role of the victim instead of relying on the respect for law that he believes to be universal: 'I have papers; I will present them with the single idea that they must be honoured'. Momentarily we recall John Proctor's stoic recommendation to Elizabeth on outfacing one's enemies: 'Show honour now, show a stony heart and sink them with it!' Monceau, however, is no Proctor, and his attitude is self-deceiving, his outward confidence masking an inner defeatism. As Leduc tells him, in one of the play's best phrases (which also has a *Crucible* ring to it), 'Your heart is conquered territory, mister' [p.191].

The contrast between Leduc's reasoned appraisal of the situation and Monceau's refusal to face the facts is valid in the historical context of the play and in more general terms. Unfortunately it would be dramatically much more effective, as a conflict, for an audience that did not bring with it to the theatre the prior knowledge that Monceau's disbelief in the possibility of the Germans committing such atrocities is entirely misplaced. Such an audience, of course, cannot be found in today's theatre any more easily than can the audience T.S. Eliot once desiderated that can neither read nor write. General knowledge, not Miller, loads the debate in Leduc's favour before it has begun. It is a problem with which the play is not strong enough to deal and, in fairness, it is not easy to see how it could.

Emphasising that *Incident at Vichy* 'is not "about Nazism" or a wartime horror tale', Miller once complained that 'a few

110

critics persist in their inability to differentiate between a play's story and its theme'.[42] The *Times* notice of the London production differentiated between them too sharply: 'As a conventional Resistance melodrama, *Vichy* holds up in the theatre. What entirely fails to come through theatrically is its intellectual content'. The story is not melodrama, the theme is more than intellectual content, and it does not help to treat the two as wholly discrete in the ways that Miller and the reviewer both do. Miller defined his aim in the play as 'to throw some light on evil'. As always in his plays (despite his afterthoughts about *The Crucible*) he has conscientiously avoided identifying totally with any one character the force of evil that the play as a whole posits. The most fully-developed of the German characters, the Major, is not the stereotypical strutting, jack-booted Nazi of melodrama. He condones the atrocities but does not initiate them, seeing himself as the victim of a kind of historical necessity in a world where 'There are no persons any more . . . There will never be persons again' [p.192] and where everyone is dominating and victimising someone else. The Major's argument is vitiated by its Monceau-like defeatism and by the drunkenness in which it is delivered; self-pity mingles contemptibly with a denial of responsibility and with the belief that love and respect are no longer possible, but he is not wholly evil.

Von Berg has to accept the fact that his cousin, Baron Kessler, whom he likes, is a Nazi implementing policies of anti-Semitism, but Leduc is brought to the realisation that Kessler 'must be a man of some kindness' to have retained Von Berg's affection. Von Berg, says Miller, 'has been, he sees, not so much an opponent of Nazism, but a vessel of guilt for its brutalities. As a man of intense sympathy for others he will survive, but at a price too great for him to pay'. The play culminates in an Ibsenite discussion between Von Berg and Leduc on whether idealism is practicable, whether it does more harm than good. Leduc defines his position.

It is not you I am angry with. In one part of my mind it is not even this Nazi. I am only angry that I should have been born before the day when man has accepted his own nature; that he is *not* reasonable, that he is full of murder, that his ideals are only the little tax he pays for the right to hate and kill with a clear conscience. [p.199].

Herein is the answer to the Major's question to Leduc: 'Why do you deserve to live more than I do?' Von Berg sacrifices his pass to Leduc partly in answer to Leduc's challenge: 'It's not your guilt I want, it's your responsibility'. Leduc is left, in Miller's phrase, to 'accept the guilt of surviving his benefactor'. Unlike the Major, he has the courage and the integrity to accept the responsibility and the guilt, as, of course, does Von Berg.

The play's moral, like the essay's, is unexceptionable, yet the play itself contradicts it. As a debate it is essentially the work of a man of reason asking his fellows to consider rationally the fact that men are *not* reasonable. That it does not come across in the theatre with complete success, however, may demonstrate the rightness of this moral: men are not reasonable enough to accept as a satisfactory theatrical experience something that is directed so primarily at their reason. In this sense the *Times* reviewer is right to stress its intellectual content as something that cannot, in the theatre, be fully grasped. Guilt, responsibility and the price men are prepared to pay for integrity are important themes to which Miller will return, but as Weatherby says in a totally different context: 'the rationalist in Miller sometimes seemed at odds with the imagination of the artist'.

9

The Price

(1)

The Price, which came four years later, is in its own unpretentious way a masterpiece. Less agonised than *After the Fall,* less moralistically ambitious than *Incident at Vichy,* it is more confirmedly domestic than either and theatrically more assured than both. No character in it can be made to bear the universality sometimes ascribed to Willy Loman as a modern Everyman; its family tensions do not arise from the public issues that troubled the Kellers. Indeed, not since the unsuccessful *The Man Who Had All the Luck* has Miller written anything so essentially private, or, indeed, a family play in which nobody comes to a violent end.

Two brothers, estranged for sixteen years, meet in the parental home to agree a price for the sale of its contents to a dealer. Rivalries and resentment from the past are revived in conversation, clarified, and brought as near to resolution as they can be, with occasional interventions from the dealer and the younger brother's wife. That is all. A cast-list of four, the entire action confined to a furniture-crammed attic, and the unity of time so meticulously observed that the first act concludes with a handshake, and the second opens as the same handshake ends. Indeed, in the 'Author's Production Note' Miller expresses a preference for a continuous, unbroken performance. Tightness of construction is matched by the taut command of the rhythms of the play so as effectively to dramatise the tensions that lie below the verbal level of the dialogue. Above all it is a *quiet* play: there are no histrionics, the characters are too civilised to lose control of their emotions and not eloquent enough to formalise them into fully-articulate debate. Yet the tension is undeniably sustained, the audience's attention securely held.

The issues are so familiar as to be almost stereotypical: the success-ethic ('Were we really brought up to believe in one another? We were brought up to succeed, weren't we?' [p.89]), the clash between family loyalty and self-advancement, the rivalry between siblings, the impact of the Depression on families of modest affluence, the inescapability of the past, the price of integrity. The dramatisation of them has obvious affinities with earlier plays, especially *After the Fall:* the father is destroyed by bankruptcy, morally as well as financially, and this is intensified for him by the loss of his wife's respect. Nobody recovers from bankruptcy in Miller's plays, and his characters are perhaps too rigidly categorised into the winners and the losers. This is not unconvincing, and it makes for effective theatre, but the criteria of moral realism by which the plays ask to be judged suggest the possibility of some financial recovery and some resilience sometimes.

Quentin's mother blamed her husband for what had befallen them; Mrs Franz, preparing, like Quentin's mother, for an important social function when the disaster overwhelmed the family, could not even voice her despair but had vomited uncontrollably over her seated husband. The violence of this image, elaborated in graphic detail by her son in his description of the incident, is particularly striking in a play that is otherwise in so low a key. In the same scene Victor sums up the meaning of the Depression in the words 'One day you're the head of the house, at the head of the table, and suddenly you're shit. Overnight' [p.88]. The expression, unexpected in Miller anyway, similarly heightens the tension by its violence. (I find it hard to understand why Clive Barnes's *New York Times* notice of the original production dismissed the language as 'pure fustian' and the central situation as 'too rigged, too pat', while epitomising it as 'good theater but not very serious theater'.)

For the two Franz sons, the father's bankruptcy has meant that funds were insufficient to support both of them through college. The younger son, Victor, therefore, was left to devote himself to supporting father, enabling the elder, Walter, to complete his course and become a successful surgeon. Quentin's professional career had been built on a similar act of altruism by his brother Dan, but in *After the Fall* that is only a minor theme. In *The Price* we are invited to contemplate the cost of such an action. Victor's satisfaction at doing what he believed to be his duty to his father had been eroded by Walter's apparent reluctance even to make a reasonable financial contribution, by his wife's increasing frustration at their restricted life-style, and by his own resentment at lost opportunity and talent under-employed. The price has been the necessity of gaining financial security by joining the police force.

Even though he had hoped it would be only a temporary expedient, the career seems odd for one whose interests and training have been in science, but the choice is not so much Victor's as Miller's. When in other plays the symbol of achievement has so consistently been a college course culminating in distinction as a lawyer, under-achievement is logically represented by this role of the enforcer of that law which he does not have the professional training to interpret or practise. The job also symbolises aptly Victor's desire to believe in a world based on order and justice.

That it involves also the wearing of a uniform identifies him publicly with his employment in a way that Esther finds distasteful, but it is consistent with Victor's willingness, like Eddie Carbone, to 'let himself be wholly known'. This is a very clothes-conscious play, for if Victor's uniform is indicative of his lack of success, Walter's clothes emphasise his professional standing. Complimented on his overcoat, he half-deprecatingly prices it at 'two gallstones'. (The phrase associates him interestingly with the impecunious medical student Quentin's mother was not allowed to marry but of whom she still thinks nostalgically when success has enabled him 'to end up so big in the gallstones'.) The real price of the overcoat, however, has been a broken marriage, a breakdown, and an evident sense of deracination. Similarly, among the relics in the attic, the father's opera-hat, the mother's gold-embroidered evening gown, and the fur lap-robe all symbolise past opulence.

In this context the comments made by all the other characters on Esther's appearance become more than conversational courtesies. Her suit, the focus of their comments, is inexpensive and 'simple' but 'really handsome': she and Victor may, in Alfieri's phrase, have had 'to settle for half' and their married life has not been easy, but she has the taste, the thrift and the pride to make the most of herself whatever their circumstances. Walter has paid, metaphorically, too high a price for his coat; the unpretentious smartness of Esther's suit is evidence of the greater stability of her marriage that is also attested by their having 'brought up a terrific boy, for one thing'. The visit to the cinema for which they leave as the play ends is a modest enough outing but at least it is a shared pleasure. Everything has its price, and nobody can expect to have everything: making the best of a bad job is the main satisfaction for which we can hope.

(2)

If I put the moral tritely this is not to belittle either it or the play, but to emphasise that the real value of *The Price* lies elsewhere. More than any of Miller's other plays, it is a kindly, understanding exploration of character and situation that proves nothing, makes no grand gestures of protest or assertion, but holds our interest simply, by saying in effect 'Look : this is how things are'. When the time covered by the play's events coincides so exactly with the two hours of its duration there can be little development of character, nor is a group so little acquainted with each other in any position to engage in character analysis. Character has to be displayed in action, yet all the significant action has taken place in the past. It is the way in which the meaning of the past changes for the Franzes in the course of their confrontation that constitutes the play's main interest, the way in which that meaning emerges that gives the play the rhythm to which I referred earlier. It is almost as though Miller has set himself the challenge 'How slowly can I keep a play moving and still hold the audience's attention?'

The curtain rises on a stage empty only in the sense that there is no human being present, for the stage direction refers to 'the chaos of ten rooms of furniture squeezed into this one . . . The room is monstrously crowded and dense, and it is difficult to decide if the stuff is impressive or merely over-heavy and ugly'. The stage is lit only slowly, as though to simulate daylight gradually creeping in. 'The room is progressively seen' and time is evidently being allowed for the audience to assimilate the atmosphere of the attic. Victor enters, and the inactivity is prolonged while he takes stock of the room, 'looks at his watch, waiting for time to pass', and eventually puts on two old gramophone records before his wife enters to find him helpless in solitary merriment at the 'Laughing Record'. A shrewd sense of timing is needed to get the best effect from this opening but it can work extraordinarily well.

The exposition scene occupies fifteen pages of dialogue between Victor and Esther in which essential information about the family background is unobtrusively conveyed. The tensions caused by Esther's drinking and by the memories of the past evoked by their surroundings are momentarily dissipated by a happier recollection, a piece of marital banter or flattery, only to surface again as the surroundings reassert themselves. Materialism is the keynote: things are in the saddle and ride the Franzes, but even more dominant is the money that the material objects represent. It is not merely that Esther urges Victor to bargain and get the right price for the household effects from the dealer, insisting repeatedly that 'There could be some real money here': sooner or later almost everything else turns to money too. The film they are to see had better be great because the tickets cost $2.50 each. Laughingly they recall 'the McLoughlin sisters — remember — with the typing service in the front bedroom?' only to translate their promiscuity into cash terms: 'In that typing service it's two dollars a copy'. Victor compliments Esther on her suit but immediately asks 'And how much?' Mention of Walter reminds them of his wealth: 'That's why he's got Cadillacs. People who love money don't give it away'. Meanwhile Victor is calculating his pension to decide whether he can afford to retire. Eventually their recognition of themselves as losers crystallises itself for Esther: 'You know what the goddamned trouble is? . . . We can never keep our minds on money! We worry about it, we talk about it, but we can't seem to *want* it. I do, but you don't' [p.21]. Yet through all their uneasiness and regrets they emerge as a likeable ordinary couple. The solidarity of their relationship is quietly established, culminating in Esther's spontaneous 'God! Victor! . . . You looked beautiful' as he momentarily recaptures his youthful fencing skill. And at once the lyrical mood is shattered by the arrival of the dealer. A short interlude in which they introduce themselves is followed by Esther's departure and the bargaining begins.

Now Victor is fencing in a way that comes less naturally than with the foil, and the second half of the act is taken up with the ritual war dance of two men sizing each other up in their desire to get the best possible price from each other. Again there is the alternating rhythm between wary tension and the relaxed banter as the two extract from each other in conversation fragmentary disclosures of their different pasts, much as Victor and Esther had alternated in the first half. Again a point of equilibrium, of shared confidence, is reached as the bargain is struck and again the mood is immediately shattered by an arrival. This time it is Walter, who was not expected. Again greetings and introductions are exchanged briefly and the act ends.

Thus the structure of Act I is simply two sustained duologues each terminated by the arrival of a new character and followed by a brief, fairly conventional, introductory conversation between three characters. Within each duologue there is an ebb and flow of mood, never extreme, but never stable for more than a few minutes before a careless phrase or a misunderstanding threatens it.

(3)

The structure of Act II is quite different. The three men on stage at the beginning are soon rejoined by Esther; from that point until the closing minutes of the play, although the dealer withdraws intermittently, the three Franzes remain together on stage throughout, piecing together their past. Here, if anywhere, the intention defined in the Production Note must be realised and judgment must be withheld 'in favour of presenting both men in all their humanity and from their own viewpoints'.

The Note requires that 'A fine balance of sympathy should be maintained in the playing of the roles of Victor and Walter' and the gradual disclosure of that part of the truth about the family past which each holds is effected with a justice as even-handed as possible. The whole that they come eventually to perceive is greater than the sum of those parts, but is not necessarily to be seen as the entire truth any more than either brother is to be seen as wholly in the right.

Miller's first-act concentration on Victor, however, predisposes us to see things from his angle. He has emerged as a fundamentally decent man who is uneasy at his inability to get the better of the dealer: the rapidity with which his outbursts of irritability are countered by good-natured friendliness strengthens our liking for him. The pace of the second act, however, is primarily determined by Walter, of whom, in their different ways, the others are all in some awe. To the dealer

Walter is a threat to the price he has offered Victor, and he cannot get Walter's measure as quickly as he could his brother's. Esther is obviously attracted to Walter, responsive to his flattery, and yet sufficiently influenced by her husband to mistrust him. As for Victor, Esther has already told him 'You're still eighteen years old with that man!' However much he resents, envies and mistrusts Walter, Walter is still his older brother: affection as well as convention make him want to respect Walter, but both the past and Walter conspire to frustrate that desire.

Walter dominates the second act because his are the more startling disclosures about the past, his mood changes more often and more sharply than Victor's which becomes rather sullen, and he seems more constructive than Victor in attempting a reconciliation. Walter's initiative in offering Victor a job in his research centre takes the audience momentarily off balance as it does Victor, but Victor's refusal of it is a characteristically realistic recognition that twenty-eight years on the beat have unfitted him, at fifty, for so radical a change; it is a response more complex than defeatism or the 'sacrificing his life to vengeance' of which Walter accuses him.

The Production Note asks us to accept that 'each has merely proved to the other what the other has known but dared not face'. Victor, however, has faced a great deal more than Walter has during the action of the play, and faced it with courage. Walter's insistence that their father still had considerable resources even after the crash and that Victor's self-sacrifice was unnecessary is a *coup de théâtre* but it does not constitute the classical *peripeteia* that it seems to promise. Victor must adjust to the full knowledge of it, and Esther to his inability to deny always having had some suspicion of it, but there is no way now in which the revelation can substantially alter their lives or the action of the play.

What Walter has learnt by the end of the play is less clearly represented. His assertion that Victor and Esther 'lay down and quit' and 'haven't the guts to face it' is called into question both by his own anger and by the dramatic action. Nor is it quite sufficient for the Production Note to put the responsibility onto the actor: 'sympathy will be evoked for him in proportion to the openness, the depth of need, the intimations of suffering with which the role is played'. Even if the sentimentalisation that this invites is avoided, the final exit speech presents difficulties. Here theatrical effect is achieved at some cost to the character, again because of his anger. Has he really faced the truth of Victor's position when he can say 'But your failure does not give you moral authority! Not with me!'? After all the mistakes Walter attributes to him, Victor's integrity has given him an authority that Walter has not acquired from his success. To an audience disinclined to see Victor as a failure, Walter's outburst may not seem wholly free from envy and vindictiveness, and to that extent he may forfeit some of their sympathy. Even if, like Sue Bayliss in *All My Sons,* Walter resents 'living next door to the Holy Family', the audience will have recognised Victor's goodness as less priggish than Chris Keller's, and the balance will tilt in his favour.

Walter is not Miller's spokesman and 'We invent ourselves, Vic, to wipe out what we know' [p.90] ought not to be taken as the play's message. Constantly the play has forced on us the question of how we can be sure of what we know: Esther voices the uncertainty more overtly than the others, but we only have Walter's testimony that there was never any love between the parents, and that their father was cynically taking advantage of Victor's generosity when he did not need it. These may be seen as partial truths — not lies, and not the self-deceiving myths Willy Loman cherished — but not the undisputed verifiable truth either. Victor's devotion to his father may have been misplaced, his motives may have been more mixed than he recognised, and sentiment may have deterred him from admitting the full implications of things he suspected. 'We invent ourselves . . . to wipe out what we know' is one formulation: 'We invent what we know to protect what we are' might be another, and both impose their price. Even if Walter commands rather less sympathy than Victor, the play does not adjudicate between them, nor does it require that we should, though the earlier Miller would have tried harder to push us in one direction or the other.

(4)

Emphasising the complementariness of the two brothers, the Production Note observes 'surely their respective psychologies and moral values conflict at the heart of the social dilemma', thus encouraging the aligning of *The Price* with the social

120

moralism of its predecessors. The difference between them, however, lies in this play's most original feature which I have deliberately left out of account in my discussion so far. In Gregory Solomon, the furniture dealer, we have the first character in a major Miller play who gives the impression of having been invented for his own sake and developed because his creator has become fascinated by him. Victor and Walter are people rather than characters, as comparison with their predecessors in the more thesis-oriented plays will show; we might usefully think of them, for example (especially in exchanges such as that at page 75), as Biff and Happy twenty years on. Gregory Solomon, however, is a character in the popular sense of the word and not merely in the theatrical sense.

The plot requires a dealer who shall haggle over the price: to make him Jewish would be tritely unremarkable, were it not for the significance with which Miller invests the fact. Solomon's accent is identified from the start as Russian-Yiddish, his idiom is equally indicative of his ethnic origins, his argument is illustrated idiosyncratically and racily. Today's consumer society wants only disposable goods, he tells Victor, because shopping is their only protection against unhappiness :

> If they would close the stores for six months in this country there would be from coast to coast a regular massacre. With this kind of furniture the shopping is over, it's finished, there's no more possibilities, you *got* it, you see? So you got a problem here. [p.38].

Even proverbs acquire a new vividness from his syntax: 'in a day they didn't build Rome' [p.92]. The markedly Jewish cadences of Solomon's speech contribute to the rhythms of the play as a whole as effectively as does the content of his speech to the play's humour, but his role is much more than comic relief.

His negotiations with Victor are amusing but their real importance lies in their expertise. Like Larry in *A Memory of Two Mondays*, Solomon is the professional in love with his work and secure in the knowledge that he does it well. The skill with which he plays, and eventually lands, the innocent Victor is admirable for its craftmanship which effectively distracts attention from its commercialism. The well-timed changes of tone, the refusal to be hurried, the threats to withdraw from the deal altogether, the reasons why some pieces are more useful to him than others, the calculated but apparently spontaneous digressions into autobiographical anecdotage, and the irrepressible resilience are a joy to observe: even Victor recognises that he is dealing with a master.

The resilience is the key to his Jewishness for, like the other Jews in Miller's work, especially the prose fiction, he is essentially a survivor. Victor's rationalisation of his father's defeat ('Some men just don't bounce, that's all') Solomon finds incomprehensible:

> Listen, I can tell you bounces. I went busted 1932; then 1923 they also knocked me out; the panic of 1904, 1898 . . . But to lay down like *that* . . . [p.41].

His longevity is in itself a sign of endurance: eighty-nine, four times married (as far as he can remember), but still sprightly as long as he is careful, and still able and willing to work. With his liveliness of mind and ready turn of wit goes a healthy curiosity: 'What happens to people is always the main element to me' [p.30] almost epitomises the play's theme. His solemn claim that, when he was president of the Appraisers' Association, he 'made it all ethical' has its comic aspect, but it is consistent with his repeated desire to conduct negotiations on a factual basis ('with used furniture you cannot be emotional'). His reminder that Walter has called the furniture 'a lot of junk' is shrewdly timed in his own business interest, but there is a hint of reproval to Walter too for his indifference to the furniture's real worth [p.56]. There is some irony in the fact that the Jewish furniture dealer is the play's most level-headed character and the one with the right values. Sharp as he is in his business dealings, there is no suggestion of unfairness: having determined the price, he sticks to it, and the basis for his calculation of it is not, as far as it is explained, unreasonable.

If in this play he represents a force for life, for continuity, somewhat as Roslyn did in *The Misfits,* it is appropriately at a level more mundane, less ecstatic, than hers, but it is also much more self-sufficient and self-sustaining. For all the clarification they offer each other, the Franzes remain locked in their past; Walter's exit does not suggest any lasting reconciliation, while Vic and Esther learn only an acceptance slightly more positive than despair. Only Solomon, at eighty-nine, can face the future with any confidence, given a new lease of life by the necessity of valuing and re-selling the furniture he has acquired. Even he has some understandable misgivings when he is left alone with his purchase, but the curtain falls as he puts on the Laughing Record and, like Victor at the opening of the play, succumbs to the infection of its laughter.

To some this has seemed to give the play an absurdist dimension, especially if it is taken in conjunction with the mention of the father's laughter, 'like it was some kind of wild joke', when asked to pay for Victor to continue at college, and with Esther's comment that 'it's all a goddamned farce'.[43] Against this has to be set Esther's final speech with its hope that 'some crazy kind of forgiveness will come and lift up everyone' and its earlier indication of her own forgiveness for all the Franzes. She has been brought to this by the realisation that Solomon's strength lies in his readiness to believe what he sees: at the beginning she has told Victor, 'God — my mother was so right! I can never believe what I see', so she has learnt something from the intervening experience. 'To admit what you see endangers principles', Quentin had decided, but it is pragmatism rather than principles that troubles Esther.

Her 'forgiveness' speech ends with the half-rhetorical question 'When do you stop being so . . . foolish?' Solomon's reply seems inconsequential :

> I had a daughter, should rest in peace, she took her own life. That's nearly fifty years. And every night I lay down to sleep, she's sitting there. I see her clear like I see you. But if it was a miracle and she came to life, what would I say to her? [p.94].

This too is a *reprise*, for he has told Victor about this in Act I, though in a less resigned mood ('. . . you can't help it, you ask yourself — what happened? What *happened*? Maybe I could have said something to her . . .') [p.42]. At the end, he still believes that he sees her, but recognises the uselessness of speculating about the past, the necessity of forgiving yourself as well as others.

Miller's affectionate respect for Solomon as a person and for his quietist wisdom does not support an absurdist interpretation of the play, and the laughter on which the play ends has to be seen in conjunction with Solomon's farewell comment to Victor who has wished him luck: 'Good luck you can never know till the last minute, my boy'. Between this and the laughter comes, according to the stage direction, a moment when 'the challenge

123

of it all oppresses him and he is afraid and worried' — a human enough reaction for an eighty-nine-year-old who has just pulled himself out of retirement. Putting on the Laughing Record steadies him: he 'shakes his head back and forth as though to say "It still works!" ': presumably a tribute to the record's sustained capacity to induce laughter, it can also imply that his own adage still works and at the last minute he again knows his good luck at being able to resume the work that he enjoys. The laughter with which he is left 'howling helplessly' is the laughter of relief, not of despair, and it is in Solomon, not in Quentin, that Miller lays the ghosts of his own past.

10

Versions of Genesis

(1)

Miller's plays since *The Price* have been his least successful in the theatre, but they are not for that reason his least interesting and it would be premature to imply an end to his career. He might have remained more in the public eye by repeating some of the formulae of his earlier success, but that has never been his way. Without capitulating facilely to new and perhaps ephemeral trends, he has still tried to break new ground with each successive play. *The Creation of the World, and Other Business* in 1972 dramatised idiosyncratically the story of Adam and Eve up to the death of Abel. To nickname it 'The Fall and After' would be to over-emphasise its links with its predecessors. It is, of course, the archetypal family drama, and it projects Miller's longstanding preoccupation with guilt on to a more theological plane, but theatrically it attempts, with some courage, rather more than that. The plot being predetermined, any originality must lie in the treatment: here, though he accepts the challenge, Miller seems less sure of himself than usual.

He is writing for the commercial theatre, not for a church festival where a 'straight' version in dignified language would be expected and acceptable. The obvious alternative is to enliven the story and its applicability to the present but without, of course, robbing it of its essential seriousness. The opening exchange sets off confidently in this direction :

> ADAM: Oh! Good morning, God!
> GOD: Good morning, Adam. Beautiful day.

Sustaining this tone successfully proves less easy.

When Marc Connelly wrote *The Green Pastures* fifty years ago he was trying, he said, 'to present certain aspects of a living religion in the terms of its believers . . . thousands of Negroes in the deep South'. In that context and at that period his unsophisticated representation of God as a Negro minister was acceptable to a white audience too, though today Connelly would doubtless be dismissed as an 'Uncle Tom'. Entering as Gabriel shouts 'Gangway for de Lawd God Jehovah!' and acknowledging the hymn that greets him by graciously commanding 'Let de fish fry proceed', God goes on to express his pleasure in the boiled custard and the ten-cent cigars he is offered, just as Miller's God approves the meat and vegetables offered to him by Adam's family: in both cases divinity manifests itself in suggestions for the culinary improvement of the offerings. Connelly's third scene opens, like Miller's play, with God and Adam bidding each other good morning: God asks 'Well, Adam, how dey treatin' you? How things goin'?', and this tone can be consistently sustained throughout a play that is all of a piece.

Because Miller is not, as Connelly was, presenting 'aspects of a living religion in the terms of its believers' he is less successful. Connelly's God can proceed to the creation of Eve by a simple rationalisation: 'Adam, you need a family. De reason for dat is in yo' heart you is a family man'. Miller's God compromises his divinity by the admission that 'you sprang out of my instinct rather than some design. And that is probably why it never occurred to me to give you a wife, you see'. The creation of both Eves is effected on stage in a very similar way, but there is one important difference. Connelly's Adam and Eve are dressed as black field-hands consistently with the child-like innocence of the whole concept. Miller's Adam and Eve, as a result of changes in theatrical convention, can be naked, but paradoxically this must jeopardise their innocence for an audience that cannot forget it is watching an actor and an actress in what is not for them, in the required sense, a state of nature. The process by which Adam and Eve become aware of their own and each other's sexuality also has to be the more explicit, and it is not easy to see how this is to be conveyed in the theatre without creating some sense of prurience and self-consciousness among the onlookers. The gynaecological terms in which God and Lucifer discuss the conception of Cain are no doubt half-humorously intended but the effect on the audience is equally uncertain.

The expulsion from the Garden involves God in the necessity of asserting Eve's inferiority: 'No more equals, you hear? He's the boss forever. Pull up your leaf. *(He turns to Adam).* And as for you, schmuck!' This male chauvinist deity with an outraged sense of modesty and a gift for Yiddish slang invective, however, launches at once into more conventionally rhetorical condemnation, 'Cursed is the ground for thy sake', in a ten-line speech printed as verse but containing such comments as 'No more living forever. You got it?'. How such shifts of tone are to be accomplished in the theatre is no easier to visualise than is the total effect that they would convey, and whether that effect would be what Miller wanted is equally imponderable.

Clive Barnes in the *New York Times* was reminded not of Connelly but of Odets's *The Flowering Peach* and Archibald MacLeish's *J.B.*: the modern playwright, he decided, 'should beware of Biblical whimsy' and he found little to say for Miller's 'comic strip version of Genesis'. Audiences seem to have agreed with him.

(2)

This is the first play by Miller in which taste and tone are so ambivalent — even ambiguous — as to baffle interpretation. The second act, in which Adam and Eve come to terms with procreation and the birth of Cain, is the most consistent. Act I, in the Garden, is the most mixed, for what seems intended to be innocently simple (the naming of animals, man's affinities with nature and with God) comes across as whimsically arch, and the Fall alternates uncertainly between tragedy and farce, while at the centre of the act is the theological debate between God and Lucifer that is perhaps the key to the play. The third act, the death of Abel, is theatrically more assured. Miller's old stagecraft asserts itself when, in the middle of a quarrel, Cain picks up a big rock only to use it, not murderously as the audience expects, but as an altar for a placatory offering to God. The alternations of mood between fear and religious faith are well handled, and there is one other well-engineered, if sensational, piece of theatre. God's reconciliation with Eve, at the end of Act II, has been signified by his joining her in 'a glorious dance all over the stage' as 'an angelic waltz strikes up': in Act III Lucifer tempts Eve into an orgiastic dance with himself, Cain and Abel (Adam trying to separate them the while), which culminates in Cain, at Lucifer's crudely-expressed command, copulating with Eve. The unexpected quiet gentleness of the God who arrives on this scene is a masterly stroke to spring on an audience awaiting an explosion of wrath.

There are good lines in the dialogue, too, if at times a little obvious, like Lucifer's question 'Do You remember the future, Lord?', Raphael's reminder 'Lord, Notre Dame isn't for six thousand years', or God's simple remark to Lucifer, 'Go to Hell!' There is an echo of Gregory Solomon in Lucifer's third-act comment on Adam and his family, 'Every time I come up here they've got more junk. What a race — a little prosperity and they don't even need the Devil'. Even neater is the exchange in which Lucifer explains his dependence on God :

> LUCIFER: But I can't — I can't *make* anything!
> GOD: Really! But you're such a superb critic.

If that is the perennial reproof of the creative artist to the theorist, a later speech of Lucifer's to God might be mischievously appropriated as a critic's explanation to Miller of the play's limitations: 'You have gorgeously pre-arranged this *entire* dialogue, and it all comes out the way You want — but You have solved absolutely nothing!' ('Mr Miller does not appear to have any enlightening answers' was Clive Barnes's formulation of this complaint.) Almost inevitably the Devil has the best part: he is a particularly persuasive tempter because of the paradoxical inversions by which Miller attributes to him the arguments one expects from God (one of the play's most effectively original devices). His first-act debate with God is also ingenious and modern in its proposal for power-sharing; the coalition would prove that God 'can love absolutely anybody' and thus 'people would never come to hate themselves, and there's the end of guilt. Another Eden, and everybody innocent again'. This speech, taken in conjunction with Cain's later recognition of their *hubris* in 'living as though we were innocent . . . living as though we were blessed!', is so close to Quentin's final denunciation of 'that lie of Eden' as to remind us that, for all its novelty, *The Creation of the World* ultimately takes us no further than *After the Fall* and is not even as compelling in the theatre.

Some critics have argued that *The Price* is so retrospective and dated in its attitudes as to suggest that it is a very early play refurbished. Its theatrical skill and assurance, as well as the

128

After the Fall: Barbara Loden (*Maggie*), (New York, 1964)

After the Fall: Jo Mielziner's set (New York, 1964)

Incident at Vichy (New York, 1964)

quiet realism of its philosophical position, mark it off for me as a real advance on the plays that preceded it. *The Creation of the World* makes greater concessions to modernity in its sensationalism of action and language, as well as in its studious avoidance of the conventions of realism, but at bottom it is a much more reactionary play than *The Price*. The Judaic-Christian framework forces Miller back into the equating of sex with sin from which his work in the 1960s ·seemed to have liberated him; his position on the good-and-evil debate and on the unregenerate nature of man seems more intransigent; and there are in the text hints of uncertainty of purpose. The uneasy fluctuations of tone are reflected in the confusions of the 'thou' and 'you' forms of address and the transcribing of certain passages as verse for no reason more obvious (or theatrically more perceptible) than that they are closer to the Biblical original than the rest.

(3)

The Creation of the World was originally intended to contain a musical element and Stanley Silverman composed settings for two songs, but after one try-out this was abandoned as inappropriate to the form.[44] The idea obviously continued to attract Miller and he returned to it in 1974. Richard D. Meyer, with whom he had worked at the Lincoln Center in New York, was by then Director of Theatre Programs for the University of Michigan at Ann Arbor and had invited Miller to produce a new play there. Not only was this, of course, the university from which Miller had received his first degree and an honorary doctorate; the universities, he now declared, had, since the 1950s, built the best theatres in the country. They contained 'an audience that was seeking rather than jaded', and 'the University atmosphere is supportive of Research, the free quest for truth . . . A professional can lift the work standards of University Theatre and receive from its audience that support for his adventure which has been all but crushed in the New York situation'. The prohibitive cost of a Broadway production, he felt, further inhibited creativity: 'frightened birds don't sing'.[45]

Miller's original intention was to put on at Michigan a new work called *The American Clock,* using a student cast, but becoming disenchanted with the script of that he laid it aside

129

and turned instead to a musical version of his Genesis play entitled *Up from Paradise*. Michigan's Professional Theatre Program funded a workshop in New York that allowed him to collaborate closely for some three months with Stanley Silverman and to assemble the professional cast that he felt this production required. One actor had appeared in *The Creation of the World;* all of them had had experience in such musicals as *Hair* and *Jesus Christ Superstar*. The production was brought to Ann Arbor for its final two weeks of rehearsal: set design and lighting were in the hands of the university theatre's own staff and the School of Music provided the musicians. Silverman produced a score and settings for twenty-two songs. Miller spoke enthusiastically of it as 'a wild kind of a thing musically . . . and every other way. It's simply a free form I feel can be very useful for the future . . . There is every style of music in it . . . blues, jazz, spiritual — every style of music, including some Monteverdi-type music that goes back to the Baroque period'. A stage-direction at one point has the angels singing '"hallelujahs" in barbershop harmonies'. Miller himself wrote the lyrics, directed the production, and also took the part of the Narrator which the rewritten script introduced.

The *Ann Arbor News,* in two notices of the play, was generally appreciative: 'with Silverman's specially created music ranging from modal to atonal, from basic rhythm and blues to electronic abstraction, the production sometimes is beautiful and shimmering'. The audience was 'charmed' and responsive to the play's wit as well as to 'the whole impressive staging', but both reviewers clearly implied reservations. One was irresistibly reminded that Shaw 'is better at this sort of thing' and thought Miller allowed his creative powers full rein only with Cain. The other found it 'an undeniably winning poetic vision of humanity' but complained that 'cerebral cobwebs still cling, and the theology is more theatrical than persuasive'. Others must have felt the same, for the New York production forecast at Ann Arbor did not materialise until 1979, and then without conspicuous success.

(4)

To speak definitively of *Up from Paradise* is clearly impossible for one who has neither seen it staged nor heard the music, but it would be only slightly more possible for one who had. 'The thing is being made at Michigan', said Miller in 1974. 'It will be changed every night probably . . . This is truly a work in progress'. It seems to have continued as such, for the typescript made available to me, with its 1978 copyright, shows further reworking and does not in all respects correspond to the original production as described by the Ann Arbor reviewers. Some indication of how that typescript differs from the printed text of *The Creation of the World,* however, may be of interest.

The story line is the same, of course, though simplified and compressed; some of the dialogue of the original is retained as well. The ambiguity of tone is much less jarring. God is rather more conventional, Lucifer much less important (though one critic observed that at Michigan the actor made 'his Lucifer more than the part dramatically sustains'). God still tells the angels regretfully that Lucifer was the only one of them capable of carrying on a conversation, but there is less evidence for this in the musical version and the reader certainly misses the almost Shavian complexity and paradox of the earlier theological debate between them. The most obvious change is the marked reduction of the emphasis on sexuality in the action, in the dialogue between God and Lucifer, and in the conversation of the mortals. This was plainly deliberate but gradual, for the typescript has no indication that Cain 'incestuously takes his mother as the devil eggs him on', which a review suggests he was still doing at Michigan.

The two versions end on quite different notes. God's branding and exiling of Cain in the earlier is omitted from the later. *The Creation of the World* ended with Eve demanding, like Esther Franz of *The Price,* 'Are you telling me that nothing *happened* here? I will not sit with you as though nothing happened!', and with Adam, before praying for mercy, telling Cain, in the tones of Chris Keller of *All My Sons,* 'Boy, we are all that's left responsible!' In *Up from Paradise* Abel's body is covered by the angels and Adam and Eve face the fact that life must go on. For Adam, Eve's latest pregnancy is a sign of hope; for her it is a cause for fear, but the curtain falls on Adam singing with obvious faith 'I know He wants us to rejoice'. (The second Michigan review speaks of 'a final oratorio joined by all that "we must choose to love or never see the Garden again" ', but this is not in the typescript.) The more severe God of the earlier play, admittedly, spoke, after the death of Abel, of having made men 'not of dust alone, but dust and love; and by dust alone they cannot long be governed', but in his next speech he realises that love is not enough: 'though the Devil himself cry peace, you'll find your war'. In *Up from Paradise,* immediately before the covering of Abel's body, the Narrator makes his final comment :

> The first funeral was that of a very young man. Now they had learned to fear, to love, to hate and to adore — had passed through every mood and motion of the human spirit, but not yet consolation — that bargaining with death, that reasoning with silence.

It is a dignified, compassionate speech as are all the contributions of the Narrator, although once the action is launched his interventions are relatively few. The recognition of the human need for consolation is welcome in a dramatist whose moral emphases have, to some, implied a detached coldness, but whether he has yet got the balance quite right is open to question.

Both reviewers' reiterated stress on the 'charm' of *Up from Paradise* imputes to the musical a blandness that these changes seem to corroborate but which the 'straight' version certainly did not have. 'After all,' Miller is quoted as telling an Ann Arbor reporter, 'the idea of a play is that you're playing. It isn't deadly. You're not in an accountant's office. It should be fun — fun for everybody, and it is now. We've got a marvellous atmosphere here'. Clive Barnes called *The Creation of the World* 'Miller's first Broadway comedy', but the comic element there jarred uneasily with the seriousness of the subject, the theological discussions, and the sporadic attempts at a more elevated poetic idiom. *Up from Paradise* is more of a piece but less of a challenge.

Having on so many occasions in this book praised the touches of humour that seemed to be increasing in Miller's work, I would have preferred to speak with more enthusiasm of his two versions of Genesis. I share the admiration of one Michigan reporter for the persistence that led Miller to a reworking of *The Creation of the World,* and even though, like most people, I am not entirely happy with either version, there are certainly good things in both: the vitality, virtuosity, and resourcefulness displayed here may be more felicitously fused on some future occasion.

11

Meditations on Life and Letters

(1)

Miller's next dramatic venture certainly did not provide that occasion, for there is no fun and little consolation in *The Archbishop's Ceiling*. Originally scheduled for production in New Haven, it was held back until Miller had done more work on it, and was eventually produced instead in the Eisenhower Theatre at the Kennedy Center in Washington; opening on 30 April 1977, specifically for only a four-week season, it has not at the time of writing, been staged elsewhere and has not been published.[46] It was unfavourably received by the *Washington Post*, the *Washington Star,* and the *Baltimore Sun*, but it should not, merely because of that, be underestimated. It re-examines, in a new context and with new emphases, themes persistently recurrent in Miller's work; it shows him experimenting yet again with dramatic structure; and its lack of success in the theatre may be attributable largely to his demanding too much of his audience or perhaps expecting an audience more sensitive in its response to tone, nuance, hint and inference than is altogether reasonable.

The setting is an unnamed central European state and most of the action takes place in the apartment of one of the characters. This is part of what was formerly the palace of an Archbishop; the baroque decoration of its ceiling makes the concealment of a microphone altogether too easy and, although its presence is never confirmed absolutely, the suspicion that it may be there conditions the behaviour of the characters and creates the atmosphere of uneasiness essential to the play's tension. The stage is set, in the most literal sense, for a political drama and had this dimension been more prominent the original audience in post-Watergate Washington might have been less nonplussed. The characters, however, are not politicians, the central issue is not political corruption, and, although it is obviously a police state, liberalism is not un-

133

equivocally presented as the necessary and best antidote. It is, in fact, much less directly political than Tom Stoppard's 1978 television play, *Professional Foul,* despite some affinities with it.

The central character is a fifty-year-old writer, Sigmund, formerly a Stalinist, who has embarrassed the current regime by a letter to the United Nations; this, because of its satiric attack on the government, has been widely noticed in the Western press. The central question is whether Sigmund should avail himself of the opportunity, which the government seems to be pressing on him, of seeking asylum abroad. He is encouraged to do so by two of his former friends, also writers: his older compatriot, Marcus, the owner of the apartment, who was imprisoned for almost five years when the Stalinists were in power; and the younger Adrian, in his forties, an American novelist with liberal ideals who has constantly tried to persuade Sigmund to take up a post in an American university. For all of them, however, the issue is complicated by Maya, poet, actress, and broadcaster, who has been the mistress, in turn, of all three, but most recently of Sigmund. Reluctant to jeopardise his marriage, he has broken with her some two months previously, but she is still deeply attached to him, solicitous for his reputation and integrity, by no means convinced that he ought to leave, and certain that the decision should be his alone. Politically her position is ambiguous; in a speech at the Cannes Film Festival she has criticised the regime and now believes herself to be under surveillance. Of all the characters Maya is the one most acutely aware of the ceiling and its implications. The only agent of the government that we see is her former husband, Martin, who is shown to have access to tapes of Sigmund's phone conversations, who manipulates the action within the play by shrewdly-timed and obviously informed telephone calls, and who, Maya believes (though again this is not established beyond doubt), controls the microphone in the ceiling.

It is the complexity of the relationships between these five characters that determines the play's outcome and ought to constitute its main interest, but the turning of the kaleidoscope requires so much of our concentration that we may become more concerned with the relationships than with the characters themselves.

Although towards the end of the play Maya professes to be puzzled as to why they have to mix their personal lives into the argument, this is characteristically one of Miller's main points: private life and public issues cannot be neatly segregated, and no motives are pure. Rivalry over Maya affects their attitudes more than they at first realise until, again towards the close, they discover that each has written a novel about her. Marcus's has been published and, somewhat to his chagrin, has attracted more popular attention than all of his more politically-committed writings. Adrian has tried to make her 'a kind of symbol of all the contradictory potentials of this country'; (to Marcus this is 'almost a very good idea' except that he believes Maya has no real understanding of what she wants). Sigmund's book, though unfinished, is the most important of the three, the one that will establish him as 'our first writer of really international scope'. The phrase is Martin's, with which the others come only reluctantly to agree, not because of political differences with Martin, or mistrust of him as Maya's ex-husband, but because he is a professional critic.

As God had ironically implied in answering Lucifer, even good critics are essentially non-creative, at least from the viewpoint of the creators, and the third strand of this play is a literary one. The question implicitly posed is whether, if Sigmund's book has so great a potential, its completion is not more important in the long term than is any political gesture he may wish to make. The play's main characters are all writers, for whom politics, sex, and art are inextricably interwoven. Professional rivalries between the men are gradually shown to colour their political judgments as much as do their rivalries over Maya, and the political significance of literature is minimised. 'I don't think a writer ought to mistake himself for an artillery regiment . . .', says Marcus, 'It's a romantic illusion that intellectuals have ever really been able to change very much by themselves . . . We can only express what is already there'; and, although he is presented as something of a dilettante, this statement goes unchallenged both by the other characters and by the action of the play. The efficacy of Sigmund's letter to the United Nations is called into question, and it is implied that the publication of photographs of him and

Maya, nude by a lake, will suffice to destroy such political influence as his literary reputation might have given him. Adrian's liberalism is discredited by his inability fully to understand the political situation and by his greater concern with self-preservation. He admits having begun as a painter, concentrating on what he calls 'high pornography' when he realised that that was what occupied his thoughts most of the time: 'Pornography is the most serious subject there is'. To all of them (though least, perhaps, to Sigmund) Maya is a sex object rather than an object of love, yet they are all obsessed with her.

Early in the play it emerges that one reason for the break-up of her marriage to Martin was his voyeuristic habits. Sigmund, recalling that it was Martin who took the photographs, remembers thinking 'how strange — that he would want to see her picture with another man, but after all . . . who is not strange?' Martin's defence of his habits is more positive: in Act I he has told Maya 'It is a profoundly human thing . . . to watch forbidden, secret acts. It may be close to the root of all art'. Miller's preoccupation in this play and others with the secret, inner springs of human conduct, as distinct from the conscious and explicable motives, gives the point some validity, as do the three men's differing books on Maya, written after their affairs with her have ended. At one level of the play Miller is obviously exploring the impulses behind literary creativity and, although no one single character incontestably embodies, in this or in any other area, Miller's own opinion, he seems to see these impulses as private rather than public and even to be uneasy about the effectiveness of literature as a means of influencing political affairs. This play probes further the idea that Von Berg had raised in *Incident at Vichy:* 'Art is perhaps no defence against [totalitarianism]' [p.171].

(3)

Martin, critic, voyeur, and unlikeable manipulator of the destinies of others, has for this play a significance quite out of proportion to the size of his part. Whether or not there is a 'bug' in the ceiling, whether or not it is being operated by Martin, the possibility of both is so real and ever-present to the others as to condition much of their behaviour. Conscious of being under surveillance, they move into the corridor for more private exchanges, or, as Adrian does on occasion, deliver to the ceiling a speech intended for governmental consumption. Maya, alone in the room, talks aloud, confident that she is thus communicating with Martin, and, adverting to his defence of voyeurism, comments 'I'm being watched now, in effect, and I can't help sort of performing'. Adrian, in a café with Sigmund, perceiving that they are being watched by two men, asks 'Doesn't it make you feel like an actor — being observed?', and Sigmund agrees: 'But of course we are all actors — the whole thing is theatre'. He repeats this idea later and at the climax of the play he develops it still further. Perhaps unexpectedly, Miller ignores the moral and political issues of 'bugging' to concentrate instead on the way in which it heightens the sense of role-playing that characterises so many aspects of twentieth-century life, reduces the gap between the public and the private self, and destroys the security of privacy on which civilisation has come to depend. Four writers and an actress are likely to be self-conscious enough by nature, sufficiently inclined by temperament to analyse themselves and each other: what the political system represented by the ceiling does is ultimately to rob them of freedom of choice by the artificial constraints to which it subjects them.

When Sigmund seems to have made up his mind to leave, the police are waiting outside. The whole experience has destroyed Adrian's confidence as well as his liberalism: concerned only for his own safety, he is contemptibly over-anxious to deny Martin's accusation that he has been subsidising Sigmund from the United States. In making the charge Martin has shrewdly coupled with it the suggestion that Adrian's Jewishness will intensify the government's paranoia and their hostility to fellow Jews like Martin within the country. Maya denies that the government is anti-Semitic ('That's Martin's neurosis') but here as elsewhere in the play the facts are immaterial: the mere possibility of it is credible and terrifying enough to Adrian. Ethnic loyalties, moral guilt, personal integrity — these have been the staples of Miller's plays throughout his career, the sheet-anchors in the storms that shake the twentieth-century seas, but here they are much less reliable. 'Maya, are you trying to drown me in guilt?', Adrian demands in near-hysteria, only to be answered with cold realism: 'But how else did you imagine it all *works?* Everyone serves'.

Both Adrian and Marcus are diminished as the play progresses, partly by their emotional instability in the face of crisis, partly by their sheer unreliability. This is achieved, however, at a cost that many would not have expected Miller to be prepared to pay: the true nature of the regime is not defined with enough sharpness, and we are in some doubt as to the extent of its iniquitousness. Marcus, for example, gives a vivid account of having been intimidated, when in London, by three men from the Embassy whose behaviour will seem to many of the audience completely and credibly in line with what they expect of such a regime; later Marcus withdraws the whole story as an impromptu fabrication. At the end it emerges that he had been denied entry into the United States in 1950 and forced to return to his own country, to be immediately imprisoned by the Stalinists: this rationalises the ambivalence of his attitude to Sigmund and Adrian but throws no light on the current regime. His denunciation of Sigmund's United Nations letter as 'a tactical monstrosity' is not categorically rejected, nor is Sigmund himself a positive enough character to convince us that he is fully justified in his stance. With Sigmund's fate uncertain, the play ends with Maya and Adrian going their separate ways, despite the entreaties of Marcus who is left discredited and alone with the Danish girl, Irena, who has been his companion throughout the play; speaking almost no English, however, she has taken no part in the action which she has clearly not even been able to follow or understand. Her role, beyond being merely decorative, seems intended to stress Marcus's womanising, but, as he has already claimed to be incapable of intercourse with anyone other than Maya, Irena's presence at the end intensifies the isolation to which his conduct has brought him. To her he dismisses what has gone before as 'Just. . . sort of a game' and the curtain falls as they kiss. This in its context is a far cry from the assertion of the need for love and consolation at the end of *Up from Paradise*. Miller's remark that 'the idea of a play is that you're playing' is less applicable here than is his other comment that 'frightened birds don't sing': beneath the archbishop's ceiling all the birds are frightened and the games that they play are fraught with menace.

Richard L. Coe, in his *Washington Post* notice of the first night, suggested that the play was 'the residue of Miller's years as president of PEN, the international writers' association'. He thought the question of the relationship between the writer and the police state was one worth raising, 'But, oh, how long it takes to get to the matter through the thickets of Act I exposition!' This, however, is to judge the play as more conventionally structured than it is. Such exposition as is required is relatively quickly conveyed, if by 'exposition' we mean giving the audience such preliminary information as it needs to pick up the threads of the action. The problem with *The Archbishop's Ceiling* is that the whole play is exposition, for it involves virtually no action and there is no *dénouement* in any tidily conventional sense. Miller himself described it as 'a dramatic meditation on the impact of immense state power upon human identity and the common concept of what is real and illusory in a group of writers living in a small European capital today'.[47] Such a concept of drama can probably be implemented with success only when the characters and their situation are of compelling interest and when the issues are such that an audience can readily apprehend them: *The Price,* after all, was effective as a conversation-piece with the minimum of action.

The Archbishop's Ceiling ought to have advantages over *The Price.* It raises issues that are larger, less narrowly domestic; more suspense is generated by the uncertainty as to whether or not the ceiling is 'bugged'; the action is, in Act I, moved in and out of the room by two devices that had worked successfully in earlier plays. Picking out a character or characters in spotlights on a darkened stage, as in *After the Fall,* enables both sides of a telephone conversation to be dramatised. As in *Death of a Salesman,* another pool of light and a table constitute a café where Sigmund and Adrian meet or a room where Martin visits Maya. Then in Act II as things close in on the group, a stricter adherence to the unities creates a suitable claustrophobia. Moreover, if in the process the audience is made to feel voyeuristic, that too is not inappropriate in this play.

If, as the reviews imply, *The Archbishop's Ceiling* makes in the theatre an impact less effective, less compelling, than Miller's other plays, there may be two reasons for it. Less sympathetic than the Franzes of *The Price,* and certainly with no Gregory Solomon among them, the characters do not sufficiently engage our interest nor do they develop in attractiveness as the play progresses. Our understanding of them depends on our understanding of the arguments in which they are almost constantly engaged, but we are likely to find those arguments insufficiently explicit to enable us readily to pick up the argument of the play. Their idiom is convincing and realistic — too much so, perhaps, because, like any group of articulate people with a background of shared experiences, they tend to rely on allusive, sometimes cryptic, exchanges that necessarily mean less to those outside the group. It is clear from the reviews that, even with the benefit of gesture, tone of voice, and facial expression, it achieves only a limited communication in the theatre. R.H. Gardner in the *Baltimore Sun* spoke of it as 'less a play than a polemic, though what its argument is remains unclear'. Careful reading and re-reading over a period of time lies behind my own commentary, and that is still tentative in many respects. I am not at all clear, for example, as to the contents of the message which Maya passes to Sigmund on a piece of paper. These are not disclosed, and Sigmund observes only that it confirms his suspicions and when, inaudibly to the audience, Maya whispers the message in Adrian's ear, his only comment, 'Oh how terrible! That poor bastard', could apply to almost any of the characters.

The Archbishop's Ceiling is a thoughtful, even an agonised, piece of writing, searching and honest as Miller's work always is. It resists short cuts and facile solutions, but it remains less accessible than one would wish, even after study of the text. It is also Miller's saddest, least hopeful, play — *Death of a Salesman* not excepted — and yet its dimensions are not fully tragic. Much of the dialogue is unusually flat for Miller, and attempts to enliven it rely at times on the four-letter crudities that may not be untypical of the characters but with which Miller has generally managed quite successfully to dispense in earlier work.

'There are no immediate plans for critical New York exposure', gloated Coe in his review, 'good news both for New York and Miller, who can now go back to Square One'. When I was writing the earlier version of this book in 1978 I was told that Miller was looking to a New York production of *Up from*

Paradise but not of *The Archbishop's Ceiling*. Visiting London in August 1979 in connection with the National Theatre's revival of *Death of a Salesman*, he told an interviewer that *Up from Paradise* would open in New York in the autumn and that he thought it might later 'go down very well' in London. He joked that 'of course it could probably be done here for about £3.50' as against the £300,000 it would cost in New York.[48] In fact, neither of these two plays has yet had a London production.

(5)

Meanwhile, in November 1978 American television screened a play by Miller entitled *Fame*. Although announced as 'a new play', it is presumably related to his piece of the same name that was presented unobtrusively in New York in 1970. Its relation to the 1966 short story, 'Fame', however, is minimal. The television piece concerns an American dramatist, Meyer Shine, coming to terms with the fame that his three successful plays have brought him. Essentially episodic, it falls into three parts. The first sees him in New York where, in a series of chance encounters, he is confronted by a succession of admirers eager to show him that they know who he is. This is more than he can be said to know, for, increasingly uncertain whether they are responding to himself, his work, or his publicity image, he finally faces his reflection in a mirror with the question 'Who are you?'

He is on the eve of departure for Italy where he is to work with an eminent Italian film director in adapting one of his plays for the screen. By nature an unassuming man, he is already apprehensive at this new development to which his fame has led. His uneasiness is increased by a well-meaning but chauvinistic friend who warns him luridly of all the perils of Europe. Consequently when, in the second part, the Italian producer's car is not awaiting him at the airport as promised, his vulnerability is intensified by his relative ignorance of the language. Having accepted a lift from a non-English-speaking Italian, he panics himself into the conviction that he is being kidnapped, only to suffer the embarrassment of discovering that the driver is yet another admirer, a teacher who respects his plays and, recognising him, has merely tried to be helpful to him. A crisis of identity followed so quickly by a crisis of communication focuses his mind sharply on the implications of fame, but worse is to come in the third part.

The Italian director pays fulsome tribute to Shine's work: 'It is the writer who is the real creator: we are only his interpreters'; but he goes on to reveal that his own interpretation in the film of *Mostly Florence* will make some changes to the original. He is accompanied by a glamorous Italian film-star who assumes, as does Meyer Shine, that she is to play the lead in this piece. It deals, Shine explains, with 'a woman of extraordinary beauty, a beauty that has astonished everyone since her childhood, and she can't help but exploit her beauty as though she were her own sort of manager, her own salesman, until she becomes quite separate from herself and can never be more than mostly Florence, not Florence altogether'. The producer has other ideas, for his Florence is to be not a fashion model but a female jockey who is superb on a horse. To Shine's objection 'But there is no horse in my script' he replies imperturbably, 'We must talk about that'. He then brings in the undersized and distinctly unglamorous lady in question. She too is American, and she eventually makes it clear that she has no intention of accepting the role but had wanted to meet Shine: her University of California doctorate had been on contemporary drama and she is, again, one of his admirers, but the most intelligent of them. She helps him, indeed, to an understanding of his own play in their discussion of it (a belated recognition by Miller of the uses of critics?). When Shine tells her 'to a great extent we are what we appear to be: we can't discount appearances so completely' she counters by referring to his confused heroine: 'her beauty is as unreal to her as it seems your fame is to you'. The play ends with Shine, back in New York, studying a photograph of the jockey: it is she who has stayed in his mind, not the Italian film-star whose Marilyn Monroe type of blonde beauty may just possibly have been a fortuitous coincidence of casting.

Fame is a light-hearted piece of which one ought not to make too much. In a short article written for the television guide Miller defined it as 'a comedy about some of the absurdities of being famous' but quickly added that 'comedy is insight' and another kind of attempt 'to come to terms with mortality'. The insight that *Fame* offers into the old debate on appearance and reality is not unconnected with one question in *The*

142

Archbishop's Ceiling: how is the public image related to the inner reality of the personality? Miller formulates this in his commentary: 'What interests me is, who is under that name? Or is there anybody at all?' John Proctor and Eddie Carbone had attached great importance to their 'name'; each in his own way had learnt the necessity of earning his 'name'. Inverting his enquiries, Miller is now concerned with the reality underlying the name that is too easily given by a gullible public and the mass media. He is prepared to admit that it may be non-heroic and even non-existent. In both *The Archbishop's Ceiling* and *Fame* this involves him in a reassessment of literature and its bearing on life. In the opening scene of *Fame* an academic tells Shine 'In your three plays we have three American classics' and the dramatist does not know what to say in reply. In the final scene he autographs a programme for a playgoer who tells him how much she has enjoyed his play. 'Good!', he tells her, 'that's why I wrote it'. Miller is evidently returning to his belief that a play should be fun.

In the commentary on *Fame* he recognises that 'Writing comedy is no joke' and finds that 'It is interesting to speculate why there is such scepticism and resistance to an artist's changing his mode or style'. His willingness, at sixty-three, to attempt such a change is a sign of continuing creative vitality. There are in *Fame,* as in *Up from Paradise,* some good things, some moments of genuine comedy, both of situation and of dialogue, and some promise. Although it is clear that he does not as yet move in this new element with anything like the expertise and assurance that he did in the old, this is no reason for scepticism or resistance. In the two plays produced since *Fame*, however, he has chosen for the time being not to exploit this vein further. Good as those plays are, one hopes that there are further changes in mode or style to look forward to. Whether or not he likes to be linked with Meyer Shine in this respect, Arthur Miller has already given us at least 'three American classics' as well as a great deal of enjoyment in the theatre and it is hard to imagine his not sustaining the versatility he has always shown.

12

The Passage of Time

(1)

Like *Fame*, *Playing for Time* (1980) was written for television but in a very different and more plangent key. It is a dramatisation of the memoirs of Fania Fénelon, the half-Jewish French singer who escaped death in the notorious Auschwitz-Birkenau concentration camp of the Second World War. The announcement that Vanessa Redgrave had been chosen to play Fania gave considerable offence to the Jewish community because of Redgrave's known anti-Israel stance and her open support of the Palestinian cause, but Miller insisted that the sole criterion must be her ability to play the part:

> To fire her now for her political views would be blacklisting. Having been blacklisted myself in time past, I have fought against the practice abroad as well as here, and I cannot participate in it now, but something more needs to be said. No actress can possibly play Fania in this play without generating the profoundest sympathy for the Jewish people, as well as a deeper understanding of some of the experiences that cried out for the creation of the state of Israel.

He speculated on whether 'the reconciling spirit had moved within her' or 'whether she wished to associate herself with the kind of statement this play will inevitably make about the Jewish people and about mankind'. He was confident that in any case 'anti-Jewish, anti-Israeli fanaticism will take no heart from this film'.[49] In the event Vanessa Redgrave's interpretation of the role was so sensitive, powerful and moving as to win general acclaim. It even led *Newsweek* to suggest that it might well be 'the finest performance ever given on a television screen', though the critic went on rightly to praise 'the ensemble acting of the fiercely dedicated cast' as well.

With a running time of 149 minutes and its locations restricted to the train to Auschwitz and the hardly less claustrophobic setting of the camp itself, the film might be expected to create an overwhelmingly oppressive atmosphere. The skilful blending into it from time to time of footage from films that were obviously shot in Auschwitz during the war heightens its unrelenting insistence on the hideous reality of the human depravity it depicts. It is a grim film, painful to watch, and yet not totally depressing. Not only the quality of the performances but also the facts of history redeem the blackness. The Nazis were defeated, Fania Fénelon survived and wrote the memoirs from which Miller took the title as well as the story. The exact extent of his debt to the original need not detain us. What he finds in it is an opportunity for exploring in greater depth and in closer conjunction a number of themes that have fascinated him throughout his career.

(2)

Prominent among these, of course, is the human capacity for survival, and his treatment of that justifies his claim for the play as a statement 'about the Jewish people and about mankind'. Here he is helped by the fact that Fania is only half-Jewish, as is Marianne, the young girl she befriends, and moreover in their first conversation they agree that 'it never meant anything' to them. In the short story 'Monte Sant' Angelo' Miller had presented survival as an attribute of Jewishness. The central character defines the whole history of the race as one of 'packing bundles and getting away', and when, in Italy, he realises that an Italian tradesman clearly has Jewish antecedents of which he himself is not fully aware, hè feels an irrational pride that 'beneath the brainless crush of history a Jew had secretly survived'.[50] Fania survives less because of her Jewishness than because of her humanity, but it is of course survival at a price, and as always Miller carefully probes the implications of that price. The conclusion to which his presentation of the issues tends, however, is not wholly to be expected.

Fania's survival is directly due to her musical ability which leads to her being chosen to join the all-women orchestra formed to entertain the German camp staff. Her moral dilemma is obvious and it is accentuated when the Camp Commandant praises her singing: 'It is a consolation that feeds the spirit. It strengthens us for this difficult work of ours' [p.58].[51] Relief at her salvation is tempered by an evident distaste for the means by which that end is achieved. She plays on—

playing for time—but courageously makes demands on her captors. Her initial consent she makes conditional on Marianne's being allowed to join the orchestra too [p.27]; she insists on telling the Commandant that her family name is not Fénelon but Goldstein [p.58]; and she tries to secure privileges for the other girls [pp.59 and 86–87]. Yet all these assertions of her independence alternate with more cautious, even obsequious, modes of address to her captors, and her insecure vulnerability is never masked. It comes as a shock to her to realise how the other internees regard her: 'I'm just not used to being hated like that' [p.52].

Even the other members of the orchestra are at times hostile to her, as on the occasion when she and Marianne are allowed to symbolise their half-Jewishness by removing half of the Star of David from their tunics [pp.77–78]. The quarrel that this provokes leads Fania to denounce the categories into which ideologies automatically force people: 'I am sick of it, sick of it, sick of it! I am a woman, not a tribe! And I am humiliated! That is all I know' [p.79]. Throughout the play Miller contrasts Fania with Esther, who plays the drums, and whom in a stage direction he describes as 'a taut, militant Zionist'. Esther's declaration, 'I am only keeping myself for Jerusalem' [p.123] has a smug fanaticism far less attractive than Fania's perplexed uncertainty. Fania sews back the half of the Star that she has removed but she does so with anger and resentment, partly at herself for needing this display of solidarity. In the screen version, at a later point in the play, one of the Polish women tries to define why the prisoners respect Fania and share their confidences with her: 'You have no ideology. You're just satisfied to be a person'.[52] The statement strikes a keynote that has reverberated throughout Miller's work, but not always with the peculiar resonance it acquires here.

Fania is also contrasted increasingly with Marianne. Captivity, deprivation and fear weaken the younger girl's character and she seeks self-preservation through prostituting herself to the Germans. Not only is her degeneration set against Fania's strength, her selfishness against Fania's altruism, but her conduct tacitly exemplifies a distinction that is always crucial to Miller: to have no ideology is not the same as to have no principles. There is in the play no overt Shavian debate on the moral issues involved, but neither is there any doubt as to the distinc-

146

tion Miller is drawing between Fania's choice and Marianne's. The high-minded question may suggest itself, 'Is not Fania prostituting herself metaphorically by joining this slave orchestra, and does not the title itself indicate that she is playing for time in the pejorative sense?' If the question does arise it is the fault of my summary which isolates themes for sequential discussion, unlike the play which deploys them simultaneously.

The conductor of the orchestra is Alma Rosé, niece of Gustav Mahler, daughter of a famous violinist, and herself an accomplished musician for whom 'Music is the holiest activity of mankind' [p.33]. Trained as a perfectionist, she insists on obtaining the highest level of performance from her players, even if in so doing she has to incur their temporary dislike. Fania's attitude towards Alma is shown as fluctuating, especially when Alma is expecting to be liberated in order to entertain German troops in other areas: to perform voluntarily in freedom the same act that she is forced in the camp to perform in captivity constitutes for Fania a moral distinction that Alma does not seem to grasp. Nevertheless, Fania always responds with sympathy and respect to Alma as an artist. Much of their conversation is epitomised in this speech of Alma's: 'In this place, Fania . . . you will have to be an artist and only an artist. You will have to concentrate on one thing only—to create all the beauty you are capable of' [p.74].

The coexistence of beauty and brutality has already been personified for Fania by the blonde Lagerführerin Mandel: 'What disgusts me is that a woman so beautiful can do what she is doing. Don't try to make her ugly, Esther . . . she's beautiful and human. We are the same species. And that is what's so hopeless about this whole thing' [p.62]. As in *Incident at Vichy* Miller wisely resists the facile temptation to make the Nazis monsters. The least human of them, Frau Schmidt, who poisons Alma rather than see her gain the liberty that the German herself so much desires, is not given a particularly prominent role. The others are partially redeemed by their love of music and other touches of humanity. Mandel is turned from a paradox into a figure of pathos by her obsession with the little Polish boy Ladislaus and the frustrated maternalism that she displays without comprehending how she has debased it by her forcible theft of the child from its natural mother. This is not love as Fania comes to understand love, any more than is

Marianne's calculated sexuality. Fania's dedication to her art is a liberating self-fulfilment, Marianne's prostitution is self-degradation. The music may give comfort to the oppressors (and the regular transformation of the orchestra into a band to 'welcome' the latest batch of internees to the camp is as distressing to watch as it is intended to be) but it also gives comfort and strength to the executants themselves.

Alma strengthens Fania's determination by telling her 'there is life or death in this place, there is no room for anything else whatever' [p.52]. In a speech that seems directly parallel to this, however, Fania reassures the young Laure, who is troubled at the realisation of her own Lesbian stirrings, 'In this place to feel at all may be a blessing' [p.96]. The sentiment carries the Miller stamp as unmistakeably as does the phrase itself. Similarly Miller's genius for the evocatively eloquent understatement is as apparent as is the 'moral' of the play in Fania's hesitant summing-up: 'All I mean is that we may be innocent, but we have changed. I mean we know a little something about the human race that we didn't know before. And it's not good news' [p.124].

(3)

Playing for Time, like John Proctor at the end of *The Crucible*, sees 'some shred of goodness' in man even after the Fall. In his most recent play Miller turns back the American clock of its title to explore once again that other fall that has always preoccupied his mind, the Wall Street crash that precipitated the Depression of the 1930s. Dissatisfied with the play in 1974,[53] he has continued to re-work it, and there are now two published texts of *The American Clock* which differ quite substantially. The observations that follow are based on the more recent, the 'final' text, published in the United States by Dramatists' Play Service and in Britain by Methuen. This text, I understand, will be used by the Birmingham Repertory Theatre for the play's first British production. I shall resist the temptation to compare it with the text published in New York in 1980 by Viking Press, except to the extent that comparison may throw light on Miller's purpose.

I must confess to some regret at the loss in the later version of Lee's earlier, period-setting opening speech, and particularly at the disappearance of his reference to the pulling down of the Sixth Avenue Elevated railway in New York City when the Rockefeller Center was built: 'They sold the whole thing to the Japanese for scrap', he recalls, and then, later in the same speech, reverts to the theme:

> Of course, some people still remember how they felt when they dropped all that stuff on us at Pearl Harbor—which turned out to be the Sixth Avenue El—but even that has evaporated and it's all turned into words.

It is entirely in character, it has an effective ironic neatness, and it encapsulates an important aspect of the play, as does the explanation of the play's title that occurred a few lines later in the original speech: 'And so we're turning back the American Clock tonight in search of those feelings that once ruled our lives and were stolen from us all by time'. The speech as a whole, however, is perhaps misleading in its slightly folksy lyricism that arouses the wrong expectation of an up-dated *Our Town*, and to expunge it is consistent with Miller's long-standing mistrust of sentimentalism.

To describe this as a play that, for years, Miller has seemed bound to write one day is not to denigrate it. His preoccupation with the Depression of the 1930s has been commented on in the foregoing pages with far less frequency than it occurs in his own, yet the reader new to Miller may have suspected me of overstating it. Here, at last, it forms the main subject of the play. Similarly, Miller's perennial concern with time remembered has already been emphasised, as has his predilection for dramatising it through the consciousness of one man. In both *A View from the Bridge* and *After the Fall* he has made use of a commentator who was also engaged in the dramatic action. Quentin had been the protagonist-commentator in *After the Fall*; so is Lee Baum in this play, but in the final text Miller enriches this device by the introduction of a second choric commentator. This is Arthur Robertson, a tycoon, whose role in the earlier version had been entirely within the action: he averts for himself by his business acumen the worst effects of the Depression, and his advice, freely offered to others from his psychiatrist to his black shoeshine man, is unwisely ignored by them. Now this role is reinforced by the choric role in which, in the present, he exchanges views with Lee on the events of the past. This additional perspective minimises the risk of the audience's uncritically accepting as axiomatic the interpretation of the past offered by only one narrator. It also provides an interesting alternative to the device of the narrator haranguing the audience in monologue, although that is not dispensed with entirely. Also, though much of the play comprises episodes recalled by Lee, several are quite independent of him, so that this is not a 'stream of consciousness', inside-of-his-head play like *Death of a Salesman* or *After the Fall*.

There is less story-line in this play than in any of Miller's except perhaps *A Memory of Two Mondays* which the author himself has called 'a plotless and leisurely play, an exploration of a mood'. He has also defined the idea that it was trying to evoke, and the terms of that definition are strikingly applicable to *The American Clock*:

> the idea, quite simply, of 'other people', of sympathy for others, and finally of what I believed must come again lest we lose our humanity—a sense of sharing a common fate even as one escaped from it.[54]

The central narrative thread is the impact of the Depression on the Baum family, and here Miller is obviously drawing to a large extent on personal memories. His autobiographical essay 'A Boy grew in Brooklyn' is especially informative in this respect. There he presents his grandfather amusingly and affectionately as something of a 'character', a 'blunt sort of Germanic business man all his life; had had a factory of importance for many years, [but] with the depression his income was gone'.[55] In the play the grandfather, reduced to having to live with the families of his two children alternately, shows in his querulousness a pathetic inability to accept the full implications of the Depression. His memories of the German people's inherent goodness deludes him into a conviction that 'This Hitler is finished', but at the same time his conservatism leads him to approve of Hitler's 'chasing all the radicals out of Germany. He wouldn't be so bad if he wasn't against the Jews'. In performance there is considerable scope for comedy in this role, partly because of his illogicality, partly because our hindsight makes his errors of judgment so clear, but there is also a deft building up of character. His resilient eagerness to find a solution to every problem is admirable, however scatterbrained his solutions seem. He deplores the time Roosevelt has to waste in fighting elections: 'I still think he's too radical, but ... if they decided to make him a king ... he could be another Kaiser Franz Joseph and the whole country would get quiet'. Similarly his temporary enthusiasm for Russia as a place where Lee might start up in business evaporates when he is told that in Russia the government owns the stores: 'The stores they own? Them bastards'.

In at least three respects Miller draws on his personal past for details of Lee's life. One dramatically effective episode in Act I is a direct and vivid re-working of this anecdote from 'A Boy grew in Brooklyn':

> I happened to have withdrawn my twelve dollars to buy a racing bike a friend of mine was bored with, and the next day the Bank of the United States closed. I rode by and saw the crowds of people standing at the brass gates. Their money was inside! And they couldn't get it. And they would never get it. As for me, I felt I had the thing licked.
>
> But about a week later I went into the house to get a glass of milk and when I came out my bike was gone. Stolen. It must have taught me a lesson. Nobody could escape that disaster.[56]

Also like Miller Lee obtains work with the WPA, though as a writer where Miller himself had worked with the Federal Theater Project. He also becomes a journalist as Miller had at one time been.

The most interesting aspect of *The American Clock* in relation to Miller's personality is the attitude of Lee to his father, Moe. In the essay Isadore Miller is presented as a man with a lively sense of humour, given to joking with the neighbourhood children as Joe Keller does in *All My Sons*. This trait is prominent in Moe too, so Miller senior may well be serving as a model. In this play, however, the old two-brothers pattern is finally abandoned and with it the father/son antagonism. In an interview in 1966 Miller was asked whether he had been very close to his father. His answer deserves quoting at length:

> I was. I still am, but I think, actually, that my plays don't reflect directly my relationship with him. It's a very primitive thing in my plays. That is, the father was really a figure who incorporated both power and some kind of a moral law which he had either broken himself or had fallen prey to. He figures as an immense shadow ...
> I didn't expect that of my own father, literally, but of his position, apparently I did. The reason that I was able to write about the re-

lationship, I think now, was because it had a mythical quality to me. If I had ever thought that I was writing about my father, I suppose I never could have done it. My father is, literally, a much more realistic guy than Willy Loman, and much more successful as a personality. And he'd be the last man in the world to ever commit suicide.[57]

This sounds much more like Moe Baum, whose buoyancy is shaken by his bankruptcy but not destroyed. The scene in which he borrows money from Lee for his subway fare and his lunch is the final, culminating episode in Act I. How Willy Loman's sons would have reacted to such a request is quite predictable. Lee's reaction is this:

> We got on the subway together and it was hard to look at one another. So we pretended that nothing had happened. But something had.—It was like I'd started to support my *father*! And why that should have made me feel so happy, I don't know, but it did! And to cheer him up I began to talk and before I knew it I was inventing a fantastic future!

This speech ends with Lee recalling how the comradeship of that occasion buoyed them both up:

> By the time we got to Forty-Second Street the Depression was practically over! (*Laughs. Music*) And in a funny way, it *was*—(*Touches his breast*)—in here ... even though I knew we had a long bad time ahead of us.—And so, like most people, I waited with that crazy kind of expectation that comes when there is no hope, waited for the dream to come back from wherever it had gone to hide.

He leaves the stage, and Act I is brought to an end by Robertson recalling his own affluent youth (a seven-figure income by his twenty-fourth birthday) and contrasting to it the condition of the thousands of people encamped at that time in shanties along the Hudson river:

> Some nights I'd go down and walk among them; remarkable, the humour they still had, and of course people still blamed themselves rather than the government. But there's never been a society that hasn't had a clock running on it and you couldn't help wondering—how long? How long would they stand for this? There were nights you could almost hear it in the air ...

The speech is dramatically important for its independent endorsement of the spirit of what Lee has just said, and for its universalising of Lee's position into the mood of the '30s.

152

Less lyrical than the other mood play, *A Memory of Two Mondays, The American Clock* is also less preoccupied with a naturalistic representation of a location. The set is described merely as 'a flexible area for actors. The few pieces of furniture required should be openly carried on by the actors ... The background can be sky, clouds, space itself, or an impression of the United States' geography'. In the New York production photographic projections on a screen at the back of the stage complemented the action with suggestions of people, places, and scenes. For all the personal elements in it, it is Miller's most deliberate attempt at a play about America. It ranges across the classes from Diana Morgan learning of the Wall Street suicide of her brother Randolph down to a prostitute and to a starving man collapsing in a relief office. Although most of the action takes place in New York, there is in each of the two acts an inset scene taking place in a distant state.

In Act I a group of Iowa farmers threatens to lynch a judge for auctioning off at a knock-down price the farm of one of their friends. One buys it for a dollar and hands it back to the owner. This does not save him from ultimate ruin and, by an elision of time characteristic of this play, we immediately see him, an itinerant stranger in New York, begging from the Baums. From this incident the boy Lee learns with perplexity that the law is not necessarily synonymous with natural justice and that the Depression may drive despairing people to take the law into their own hands. In Act II, an older man, and working on a Mississippi steamboat, he sees the Depression reduce the law, in the shape of a Southern Sheriff who has received no pay for three months, to using a radio as currency in order to obtain from a black a ten-dollar fried chicken dinner with which to be able to ingratiate himself with an influential relative. As the black phlegmatically observes to Lee, 'the main thing about the Depression is that it finally hit the white people. 'Cause us folks never had nothin' else.'

This is essentially an episodic play, with a cast list of more than forty characters, though by doubling the New York production managed with only fifteen players. Not having yet seen the play in performance, I do not know whether this multiplicity of characters would confuse the audience as I feared might happen, with a significantly smaller number, in *After the Fall*.

At least the self-contained nature of each episode limits the number on stage at any one time and obviates the difficulties created in *Incident at Vichy*.[58] The cliché of 'a crowded canvas' comes too readily to mind, and indeed the Viking text is subtitled 'A Mural for Theatre'. It might lend itself more readily to television than to the theatre, but in conception it seems to me to owe much to the WPA Living Newspaper which Miller himself has said 'created perhaps the only new form invented in America, holding up the social system as such to inspection. When WPA died, the threat of the masses entering the theatre receded'.[59]

The American Clock may not bring the masses back into the theatre, but the form its social comment takes should not alienate them. It has a strong documentary quality with its use of the popular songs of the period and its references to film stars, politicians, sportsmen and other well-known figures. There are mentions of Scott Fitzgerald and Hemingway, but not of writers like John Dos Passos, James T. Farrell or John Steinbeck. Yet it is of Steinbeck that one is often reminded: by the farmers' scene, for example, by the play's general attitude, and most when the starving man in the relief centre is revived with a baby's bottle of milk in a way that recalls the more sensational incident at the end of *The Grapes of Wrath*. When the sheriff's radio is switched on it conveniently picks up a Roosevelt speech urging that government be given 'the vibrant personal character that is the embodiment of human charity'. A 'vibrant personal character' is what *The American Clock* itself aims at.

Consistent with its documentary emphasis it alludes to what was happening at the time in Hitler's Germany and Mussolini's Italy, it represents the views of a young Marxist and of a labour organiser from the Workers' Alliance. It includes in a minor role an immigrant xenophobic demagogue who insists that the word 'democracy' never occurs in the Constitution and that Roosevelt was sworn in on a Dutch bible. At one point, however, Robertson soliloquises:

> I catch myself feeling smug about the tremendous number of extremist crusades that came roaring down the runway, but never took off. Furious, cruel-talking haters of labour, Jews and blacks and foreigners. Sometimes the political air could stink with hate. And worst of all, after two years or so, you knew that no one really had a solution to this crisis.

Edie, the Marxist, makes a living writing dialogue for the *Superman* comic strip, convinced that 'Superman is one of the greatest teachers of class consciousness'. When she complains of the backwardness of the workers Lee tells her:

> They're not backward, they're normal. Normally anti-Semitic, anti-Negro, and anti-Soviet. They're building unions and that's good, but inside their heads it's full of fascism.

However, since he is also physically attracted to her, she dismisses him because 'you make everything trivial . . . you have no real faith in anything . . . you are not a good person'.

Lee's last speech in the play would doubtless confirm Edie's misgivings for her. His most vivid memory is ultimately a quixotic one of his mother:

> In her own crazy way she was so much like the country. There was nothing she believed that she didn't also believe the opposite. . . . I'd come home and give her a real bath of radical idealism and she was ready to storm the barricades; by evening she'd fallen in love again with the Prince of Wales. . . With all her defeats she believed to the end that the world was meant to be better.—I don't know; all I know for sure whenever I think of her, is that I always end up—with this headful of life!

For Lee it all comes back to people, to individuals, in the end. In the earlier text this was established so plainly in the opening soliloquy that its subsequent omission is explicable in the interest of delaying its impact. (My impression from reading the two versions is that, in general, the earlier is the less dramatically effective; for example, the farm auction is only reported there, whereas here it is dramatised in a vivid little vignette.)

The later text opens with a much shorter soliloquy by Lee, expressing his fear that the Depression could recur: 'suddenly, without warning, it may all fall apart again'. At once Robertson enters and rejects that possibility: 'People are a lot more sophisticated now, they expect ups and downs, they are much more sceptical'. Similarly Lee's closing soliloquy, with which the earlier version had ended, is now followed immediately by Robertson who is given the last word. He reiterates his beliefs that the Depression is unlikely to recur, but weakens it slightly by adding 'but of course there is no limit to human stupidity'. His concluding words sum up the role of Franklin D. Roosevelt:

In truth, he was a conservative, traditional man who was driven to the Left by one emergency after another... But willy-nilly, the net result of all his floundering, his experimentation, his truth-telling and his dire prevarications—was that the people came to believe that the country actually belonged to them. I'm not at all sure that this was his intention; I'm not even certain exactly how it came to be, but in my opinion—that belief is what saved the United States.

A cautious, temperate, non-ideological conclusion tinged with a gentle irony, this is completely consistent with the whole tenor of Miller's later work.

(5)

Readers familiar with Miller's work will readily find in these last two plays more parallels with and echoes of the earlier plays than I have felt it necessary to enumerate here. The big themes of personal responsibility, guilt, the relation between the microcosm of the family and the macrocosm of modern society, the effect of the passing of time on memory and on perspective, the moral stance and value of protest, public and private integrity, all these recur. There are parallels among and interesting variations on characters and situations throughout the canon, even down to minor details. When Mrs Baum is forced to contemplate pawning her pearl necklace Lee remarks with misplaced optimism 'Don't you love Brooklyn, Ma? We ought to plant some kind of fruit tree in the backyard. Imagine, go out and pick an apple or something?': its sentiment and its untimeliness immediately recall Willy Loman with his flash-light and his packet of seeds.

The first American production of *The American Clock* provoked in several critics reflections of this nature, usually expressed with unsympathetic and gloating self-righteousness. One took the opportunity of dismissing Miller as 'a one-subject dramatist, and that one subject found its luckiest form in *Death of a Salesman*'. He even went on to resurrect the tired arguments that *Death of a Salesman* 'is much closer to melodrama than to the tragedy it aspires to' and that 'Miller, alone among putatively major playwrights, has no language'. It is a truism that, nowadays especially, when a writer has over a period of years established a reputation for himself, it is fashionable to denigrate him as so far from *avant-garde* as to have become *passé*. To belittle *The American Clock* in this way withou recognising the advances it makes in technique and in thought on its predecessors is particularly imperceptive.

It will not be the theatrical landmark that some of his other plays have been, and the qualified faith it expresses in 'the people', balanced by its rejection of ideologies and its sober acceptance of the imperfections of individuals, will be too readily scorned by the committed. Nevertheless, there may prove to be an audience still for drama that sees human life as a matter of survival, of coming to terms, and of making the best of circumstances not of your choosing, while at the same time demonstrating 'some shred of goodness' in flawed humanity.

The mistrust of ideology in these two plays is not new: Miller's attitude towards it has always been healthily and increasingly sceptical. *Playing for Time* has been seen by some as a denial of any social impact to art because the musicians are concerned only with self-preservation. This is to force the play into altogether too rigidly symbolic a framework. Music is after all the form of art that least lends itself to social comment, and the value of the comment that the play itself makes on the holocaust is unmistakeable. To the extent that any philosophy of art may be inferred from that play, it is that art, in addition to what it does for the audience, has for the artist himself a significance that may well be therapeutic. I see *Playing for Time* and *The American Clock* as representing for Miller a release from two deeply-felt concerns that have preoccupied him for much of his creative life. Those concerns, that culminate here in two very effective plays, have never prevented him from developing successfully a wide range of other themes and other forms, and I see in the dramatic resolution of those two concerns now no grounds whatever for regarding Miller as a spent force.

Notes

1. 'The Family in Modern Drama', *Atlantic,* cxcvii (April 1956), pp.35-41; 'On Social Plays', *A View from the Bridge* (two-act version, 1957), Cresset Press (London) edition, pp.7–24. These and Miller's other occasional critical essays (including the whole of the Introduction to *Collected Plays*, 1957) have now been collected in *The Theater Essays of Arthur Miller*, 1978, and, unless otherwise indicated, page references in these Notes will be to that book. In the text of the present work, however, where reference is made from time to time to both the Introduction and the text of *Collected Plays* 1957, it has seemed preferable to retain the original references to that volume.

2. *The Portable Arthur Miller* edited, and with an Introduction, by Harold Clurman, (New York, Viking Press, 1971), p.xxiii.

3. The review was by T.C. Worsley in *The New Statesman and Nation,* 6 August 1949, pp.146-7. Miller's comment is in *Theater Essays*, p.148. Unless otherwise indicated, all Miller's comments on his own plays quoted in the text of the present book will be found in the Introduction to *Collected Plays*. In a 1966 interview Miller revealed that 'much of *Death of a Salesman* was originally written in verse'. See *Theater Essays*, pp.277–278.

4. The comments quoted in these two paragraphs will be found in the following: Harold Hobson, *The Theatre Now,* (London, Longmans Green, 1953), p.122; *The Sunday Times,* 31 July 1949, p.2; Kenneth Tynan, 'American Blues', *Tynan on Theatre* (Harmondsworth, Penguin Books, 1964) pp.140-50; (subsequent quotations from Tynan also come from this book); W.J. Weatherby, *The Guardian,* February 1968. The whole subject is more extensively considered in my essay, '*Death of a Salesman* in England', in *The Merrill Studies in Death of a Salesman,*

compiled by Walter J. Meserve (Columbus, Ohio, Merrill Publishing Co., 1972), pp.8-17.

5. Quoted in *Best Plays 1948-9*, pp.53-4.

6. Mary McCarthy, *Sights and Spectacles 1937-1958* (London, Heinemann, 1959), pp.xxiv-xxv; Henry Popkin, 'Arthur Miller, The Strange Encounter', *The Sewanee Review,* LXVIII (1960), p.37. (Subsequent quotations from Popkin also come from this article).

7. In *Holiday,* XVII, (March, 1955). See also 'The Shadows of the Gods' *Harper's Magazine* (August, 1958) (*Theater Essays*, pp.175–194) from which the quotations are taken.

8. Unless otherwise indicated all page references following quotations from Miller's plays relate to the Penguin editions listed in the Bibliographical Note at pp.169–70.

9. David Riesman, Nathan Glazer, and Reuel Denney, *The Lonely Crowd,* New Haven, Yale University Press, 1950.

10. This and the other critical comments by Miller quoted in this section are to be found in *Theater Essays*, pp.16–21. See also his comments on Ibsen in the introduction to *Collected Plays*.

11. For comparative purposes the translation cited is that of R. Farquharson Sharp in the Everyman Library (London, 1911).

12. Joseph Wood Krutch, *American Drama Since 1918,* rev. edn., New York, 1957, p.325.

13. Harold Hobson, *The Theatre Now* (1953), p.125. The quotation that follows this is from his *Sunday Times* review. See also note 4 above and the photographs facing p.33.

14. Philip Hope-Wallace reviewed it in *The Manchester Guardian* on 30 July 1949 and *Time and Tide* 6 August; Audrey Williamson wrote on it in *Theatre of Two Decades* (London, Rockliff, 1951).

15. *Drama,* (Winter, 1949), p.8. Trewin also reviewed it in *The Illustrated London News,* 27 August 1949.

16. Eric Keown, *Punch,* 10 August 1949.

17. *Theatre Arts,* November 1949, p.13.

18. *Tulane Drama Review* II (May, 1958), pp.63-9. The passage quoted should be compared with the parallel passage in *Theater Essays*, p.148.

19. *Tulane Drama Review,* May, 1958, p.66.
20. Daniel E. Schneider, 'Play of Dreams', *Theatre Arts,* October, 1949, pp.18-21.
21. *Theatre Arts,* October 1953, p.34.
22. 'The Family in Modern Drama', *Theater Essays,* p.80.
23. Both statements will be found in *Twentieth Century Interpretations of The Crucible,* edited John H. Ferres (Prentice Hall, New Jersey, 1972).
24. Quoted by Krutch, *American Drama Since 1918,* p.325.
25. *Theater Essays,* pp.17–18.
26. Interview in *Theatre Arts,* October, 1953.
27. The text was published in *Theatre Arts,* October 1953, and reprinted in Ferres, *op. cit.* Much of the information in this chapter about productions of the play derives from the *Theatre Arts* feature. The scene was also included in the acting edition (New York, Dramatists Play Service, 1954).
28. The 1954 acting edition referred to in note 27 seems to be the only edition to correct these errors.
29. Quoted by John Chapman (no source given) in *Theatre '56* (New York, 1956). For the text of the first version of the play I have depended on the abridgements published here and in *The Best Plays of 1955-56* (New York, Dodds, Mead & Co., 1956).
30. The New York City Youth Board in 1955 commissioned Miller to write a film script illustrating its work with street gangs but cancelled the contract when he came under Congressional investigation.
31. *Theater Essays,* pp.6–7.
32. Louis Kronenberger, *Best Plays of 1955-56,* p.13.
33. See, e.g., Raymond Williams, 'The Realism of Arthur Miller', *Critical Quarterly,* 1959; Henry Popkin, 'Arthur Miller: The Strange Encounter', *Sewanee Review,* 1960; Albert Hunt, 'Realism and Intelligence: Some Notes on Arthur Miller', *Encore,* 1960; and my own *Arthur Miller,* Oliver and Boyd, 1961.
34. *Harper's Magazine,* November 1960, p.66. *Theater Essays,* p.227.
35. In an interview with W.J. Weatherby, *The Guardian,* 3 November 1960.
36. W.J. Weatherby, *Conversations with Marilyn,* London,

Robson Books and Sphere Books, 1976. All subsequent attributions to Weatherby are to this book. A more detailed account of the making of *The Misfits* and the break-up of the marriage will be found in the following books: James Goode, *The Story of The Misfits,* Indianapolis, Bobbs-Merrill, 1963; Fred Lawrence Guiles, *Norma Jean: the Life of Marilyn Monroe,* New York, McGraw-Hill; London, W.H. Allen, 1969; Mayflower Books (paperback) 1971.

37. Frank Lawrence Guiles (*op. cit.*) instances a number of other such parallels. For the Barbara Loden/Marilyn Monroe resemblance see the photograph facing p.128 of the present book.

38. When Maggie wishes to annoy Quentin she calls him 'Judge' or 'Judgey'. It is at once a sneer at his profession, a hint at the play's moral theme, and perhaps an allusion to this incident.

39. 'The worst corruption of all is when the best are corrupted'.

40. The notes are reproduced, with two essays by Clurman, in *Arthur Miller: A Collection of Critical Essays,* edited Robert W. Corrigan, Prentice Hall, New Jersey, 1969. Further references to Clurman below relate to these sources.

41. The Penguin text, to which page references are given, is in *New American Drama,* Penguin Plays PL 66, Harmondsworth, 1966.

42. In *The Best Plays of 1964-65* (Burns Mantle Yearbook) pp.227-8. Further quotations from Miller in this chapter are from this source.

43. See, e.g. Ralph Willett, 'A Note on Arthur Miller's *The Price*', *Journal of American Studies* vol. v, December 1971.

44. Much of the information in this section is based on cuttings from the *Ann Arbor News* of 21, 24 and 26 April 1974, the programme for *Up from Paradise,* and a letter from J. Roland Wilson, General Manager of the Professional Theatre Program of the University of Michigan. I am grateful to Mr Wilson and to Harriet C. Jameson, Head of the Rare Books and Special Collections Department of the University of Michigan Library, for

these. For the typescript of *Up from Paradise* (copyright 1978) and for much other help I am greatly indebted to Mr Miller and his agent, Katharine Brown, of International Creative Management, New York.

45. Miller's hostility to New York here is no doubt connected, at least in part, with the disillusion he had expressed in the *New York Times* in April 1972 with the policy of the Lincoln Center (see 'Arthur Miller vs. Lincoln Center', *Theater Essays*, pp.354–361; pp.315–317 also refer).

46. Again, I am very grateful to Mr Miller and his agents for providing me with a typescript.

47. *New York Times*, 3 May 1977.

48. London *Evening Standard*, 30 August 1979, p.14.

49. All the passages quoted appear in a piece by Richard F. Shepard in the *New York Times*, 8 Aug. 1979.

50. This story, already mentioned at p.88, was first published in *Harper's Magazine*, March 1951, pp.39–47, and reprinted in the collection of Miller's short stories, *I Don't Need You Any More* (Viking, 1967, Bantam Books, 1968). 'Brainless' in the second quotation replaces 'glacial' in the original 1951 text.

51. Page references cited are to the Bantam Books edition of this play (New York, 1981). This text differs in a number of respects from the version screened: the opening is slightly different and the film ends with the liberation of the prisoners whereas the text has a coda set in 1980 which adds little to the drama and might well seem anticlimactic in performance. Some sequences seem to occur at different points in the two versions. See also Note 52.

52. This speech, transcribed as heard in the screen version, does not occur in the book.

53. See p.129 above.

54. *Theater Essays*, p.260.

55. See also p.18 and note 7 above.

56. As well as appearing in 'A Boy grew in Brooklyn', this incident occurs again in 'The Shadows of the Gods' (1958) in this form. *Theater Essays*, pp.176–177.

57. *Theater Essays*, pp.267–268. The connections between *The American Clock* and the Miller family are strengthened by the fact that in the American production the role of the mother was played by Miller's actress-sister,

Joan Copeland, apparently at Miller's suggestion (*New York Times*, 16 Nov. 1980).

58. See pages 91 and 106–107 for my comments on the two earlier plays.

59. *Theater Essays*, p.349.

American and British Premieres of Miller's Plays and Films

1936 **Honors at Dawn**
USA: University of Michigan, Ann Arbor. Avery Hopwood Drama Award.

1937 **They Too Arise** (originally entitled *No Villain*)
USA: Lydia Mendelssohn Theatre, Ann Arbor, 12 and 13 March. The Hillel Players, directed by Frederic O. Crandall. 3 performances. Avery Hopwood Drama Award and Theatre Guild Bureau of New Plays Award.

1944 **The Man Who Had All the Luck**
USA: Forest Theatre, New York, 23 November. Produced by Herbert H. Harris, directed by Joseph Fields, settings by Frederick Fox. Karl Swenson as David Beeves, Eugenia Rawls as Hester, Jack Sheehan as Patterson Beeves. 4 performances. Theatre Guild National Prize.
UK: Tower Theatre, Canonbury, London, 28 April 1960. Presented by In-Stage, directed by Charles Marowitz, designed by John Stokes.

1947 **All My Sons**
USA: Coronet Theatre, New York, 29 January. Produced by Harold Clurman, Elia Kazan and Walter Fried, in association with Herbert H. Harris; directed by Elia Kazan, setting by Mordecai Gorelik. Ed Begley as Joe Keller, Beth Merrill as Kate, Arthur Kennedy as Chris, Lois Wheeler as Ann. 328 performances. New York Drama Critics' Circle Award.
UK: Lyric Theatre, Hammersmith, 11 May 1948, transferred to the Globe Theatre London 19 June. Tennent Production. Joseph Calleia as Joe, Margalo Gillmore as Kate, Richard Leech as Chris, Harriette Johns as Ann. 111 performances.
FILM VERSION: Universal International production for General Film release, 1948. Directed by Irving Reis with Edward G. Robinson as Joe and Burt Lancaster as Chris.

1949 **Death of a Salesman**
USA: Morosco Theatre, New York, 10 February.
Produced by Kermit Bloomgarden and Walter Fried,
directed by Elia Kazan, setting by Jo Mielziner,
incidental music by Alex North. Lee J. Cobb as Willy,
Mildred Dunnock as Linda, Arthur Kennedy as Biff,
Cameron Mitchell as Happy. 742 performances. Pulitzer
Prize, New York Drama Critics' Circle Award, etc. UK:
Phoenix Theatre, London, 28 July, directed by Elia
Kazan, setting by Jo Mielziner. Paul Muni as Willy,
Katharine Alexander as Linda, Kevin McCarthy as Biff,
Frank Maxwell as Happy. 204 performances.
FILM VERSION: Stanley Kramer Company production for
Columbia release, 1952. Directed by Laszlo Benedek.
Fredric March as Willy, Mildred Dunnock as Linda,
Kevin McCarthy as Biff, Cameron Mitchell as Happy.

1950 **An Enemy of the People**
USA: Broadhurst Theatre, New York, 28 December.
Produced by Lars Nordenson, directed by Robert Lewis,
settings by Aline Bernstein. Fredric March as Dr.
Stockmann, Florence Eldridge as Mrs Stockmann,
Morris Carnovsky as Peter Stockmann. 36 performances.

1953 **The Crucible**
USA: Martin Beck Theatre, New York, 22 January.
Produced by Kermit Bloomgarden, directed by Jed
Harris, settings by Boris Aronson. Arthur Kennedy as
John Proctor, Beatrice Straight as Elizabeth, Madeleine
Sherwood as Abigail, Jenny Egan as Mary Warren, E.G.
Marshall as Hale. 197 performances. Antoinette Perry
Prize, Donaldson Prize, and runner-up for the New York
Drama Critics' Circle Award. The additional
Proctor/Abigail scene in the wood (see p.64) was
introduced into this production towards the end of its run.
UK: Theatre Royal, The Bristol Old Vic, 9 November
1954. Directed by Warren Jenkins, settings by Patrick
Robertson. Edgar Wreford as John Proctor, Rosemary
Harris as Elizabeth, Pat Sandys as Abigail, Perlita
Neilson as Mary Warren, Michael Allinson as Hale. 22
performances (normal repertory run). The additional
'wood' scene was included in this production.
FILM VERSION: *Les Sorcières de Salem* (English title *The*

Witches of Salem, American title *The Crucible*). Films-Borderie production for Films de France release, 1957. Script by Jean-Paul Sartre. Directed by Raymond Rouleau, photography by Claude Renoir. Yves Montand as John Proctor, Simone Signoret as Elizabeth, Mylene Demongeot as Abigail.

1955 **A Memory of Two Mondays** and **A View from the Bridge** (double bill of two one-act plays).

USA: Coronet Theatre, New York, 29 September. Produced by Kermit Bloomgarden and Whitehead Stevens, directed by Martin Ritt, settings by Boris Aronson. In *A Memory of Two Mondays* Leo Penn as Bert, Van Heflin as Larry, J. Carrol Naish as Gus. In *A View from the Bridge* Van Heflin as Eddie, Eileen Heckart as Beatrice, J. Carrol Naish as Alfieri, Gloria Marlowe as Catherine. 149 performances.

UK: Playhouse, Nottingham, 29 September 1958. Directed by Val May, setting by Mark King. Terry Scully as Bert, Bryan Pringle as Larry, James Cossins as Gus. 16 performances (normal repertory run).

1956 **A View from the Bridge** (two-act version).

UK: Comedy Theatre, London, 11 October. Produced by the New Watergate Club, directed and designed by Peter Brook. Anthony Quayle as Eddie, Megs Jenkins as Beatrice, Michael Gwynn as Alfieri, Mary Ure as Catherine. 220 performances.

FILM VERSION: Transcontinental production for Paramount release, 1961. Directed by Sidney Lumet. Raf Vallone as Eddie, Maureen Stapleton as Beatrice, Morris Carnovsky as Alfieri, Carol Lawrence as Catherine.

1961 **The Misfits** (film)

Seven Arts production for United Artists release. Produced by Frank E. Taylor, directed by John Huston, music by Alex North. Clark Gable as Gay, Marilyn Monroe as Roslyn, Montgomery Clift as Perce.

1964 **After the Fall**

USA: presented by the Lincoln Center Repertory Theatre at the ANTA-Washington Square Theatre, New York, 23 January. Produced by Robert Whitehead, directed by Elia Kazan, designed and lit by Jo Mielziner. Jason Robards as Quentin, Barbara Loden as Maggie,

Salome Jens as Holga. 59 performances.

UK: presented by the Belgrade Theatre Trust at the Belgrade Theatre, Coventry, 31 October 1967. Directed and designed by Leonard Schach. Leon Gluckmann as Quentin, Erica Rogers as Maggie, Marika Mann as Holga. 15 performances (normal repertory run).

1964 Incident at Vichy

USA: presented by the Lincoln Center Repertory Theatre at the ANTA-Washington Square Theatre, New York, 3 December. Directed by Harold Clurman, setting by Boris Aronson. David Wayne as Von Berg, Joseph Wiseman as Leduc. 99 performances. (Illustration 00).

UK: Theatre Royal, Brighton, 10 January 1966, transferring to the Phoenix Theatre, London, 26 January. Directed by Peter Wood, setting by Rolf Gerard. Alec Guinness as Von Berg, Anthony Quayle as Leduc. 91 performances.

1968 The Price

USA: Morosco Theatre, New York, 7 February. Produced by Robert Whitehead, directed by Ulu Grosbard, setting by Boris Aronson. Pat Hingle as Victor, Kate Reid as Esther, Harold Gary as Solomon, Arthur Kennedy as Walter. 425 performances.

UK: Duke of York's Theatre, London, 4 March 1969. Directed by Arthur Miller, setting by Boris Aronson. Albert Salmi as Victor, Kate Reid as Esther, Harold Gary as Solomon, Shepperd Strudwick as Walter. Ran 51 weeks until 14 February 1970 (theatre record).

1970 Fame and The Reason Why (double bill of two one-act plays)

USA: The New Theater Workshop, New York. With Eli Wallach and Anne Jackson. Productions at the Workshop are usually mounted for not more than three performances and are not publicly advertised.

1972 The Creation of the World, and Other Business

USA: Shubert Theatre, New York, 30 November. Produced by Robert Whitehead, directed by Gerald Freedman, setting by Boris Aronson. Stephen Elliott as God, George Grizzard as Lucifer, Bob Dishy as Adam, Zoe Caldwell as Eve, Barry Primus as Cain. 20 performances.

UK: Nicolson Square Theatre, Edinburgh, 17 August 1974. Produced by Tangent Theatre Company, West Midlands, on the Edinburgh Festival Fringe. 14 performances.

1974 **Up from Paradise**

USA: The Power Center for the Performing Arts, University of Michigan, Ann Arbor, 23-28 April. Presented by the University of Michigan Theatre Programs, directed by Arthur Miller, music by Stanley Silverman, musical direction by Roland Gagnon. Bob Bingham as God, Larry Marshall as Lucifer, Allan Nicholls as Adam, Kimberly Farr as Eve, Seth Allen as Cain.

1977 **The Archbishop's Ceiling**

USA: Eisenhower Theatre in the Kennedy Center, Washington, D.C., 30 April — 28 May. Directed by Arvin Brown, setting by David Jenkins. John Cullum as Sigmund, Bibi Anderson as Maya, Douglas Watson as Marcus, Tony Musante as Adrian.

1978 **Fame** (television)

NBC, 30 November. Richard Benjamin as Meyer Shine, Jose Ferrer as Francesco, Shera Danese as Lucia, Linda Hunt as Mona.

1980 **The American Clock**

USA: opened at the Spoleto Festival's Dockside Theatre in Charleston, South Carolina, on 24 May after 21 previews at the Harold Clurman Theatre in New York. Returned to New York to the Biltmore Theatre on 20 November, directed by Vivian Matalon (the earlier production had been directed by Daniel Sullivan), setting by Karl Eigsti. John Randolph as Moe, Joan Copeland as Rose, and William Atherton as Lee (this role had been played in the earlier production by Peter Evans).

UK: scheduled to open at the Birmingham Repertory Theatre on 18 April 1983 (with previews from 15 April), running till 14 May.

1980 **Playing for Time** (television) CBS, 30 Sept. 1980. Vanessa Redgrave as Fania Fénelon, Jane Alexander as Alma Rosé, Shirley Knight as Lagerführerin Mandel. Transmitted in the UK on the Independent Television Network by London Weekend Television 11 January 1981.

Bibliographical Note

(a) PLAYS BY ARTHUR MILLER

The Man Who Had All the Luck. In *Cross-Section: A Collection of New American Writing*, edited by Edwin Seaver. New York: Fischer, 1944.

All My Sons. New York: Reynal & Hitchcock, 1947. Harmondsworth: Penguin, 1961 (with *A View from the Bridge*). Previous English publication in *Collected Plays* (1958).

Death of a Salesman. New York: Viking; London: Cresset, 1949. (With expanded initial description and stage directions, New York: Bantam Books, 1951, and Viking Compass Books, 1958). Harmondsworth: Penguin, 1961.

An Enemy of the People (adaptation of Ibsen's play). New York: Viking, 1951. London: in *Four Plays of Our Time*, edited by H. Voaden, Macmillan, 1960. Harmondsworth: Penguin, 1977.

The Crucible. New York: Viking, 1953. London: Cresset, 1956. Harmondsworth: Penguin, 1968. Also, with an additional scene (subsequently omitted), in *Theatre Arts*, October 1953, and New York: Dramatists' Play Service, 1954.

A View from the Bridge and *A Memory of Two Mondays*. New York: Viking, 1955 (as two one-act plays).

A View from the Bridge (two-act version). New York: Dramatists' Play Service, 1957. London: Cresset (with an essay 'On Social Plays'), 1957. Harmondsworth: Penguin, 1961 (with *All My Sons*).

Collected Plays (with an Introduction). New York: Viking, 1957. London: Cresset, 1958; Secker & Warburg, 1974. Contains *All My Sons* (first English publication), *Death of a Salesman*, *The Crucible* (final text), *A Memory of Two Mondays* (only English publication), and *A View from the Bridge* (two-act version).

After the Fall. New York: Viking, 1964. London: Secker & Warburg, 1965. Harmondsworth: Penguin, 1968.

Incident at Vichy. New York: Viking, 1965. London: Secker &

Warburg, 1966. Also in *New American Drama*, Harmondsworth: Penguin, 1966.

The Price. New York: Viking; London: Secker & Warburg, 1968. Harmondsworth: Penguin, 1970.

The Creation of the World, and Other Business. New York: Viking, 1973.

Collected Plays. Volume Two. New York: Viking, 1981. London: Secker & Warburg, 1981. Contains *The Misfits, After the Fall, Incident at Vichy, The Price, The Creation of the World, and Other Business* and *Playing for Time*.

Playing for Time. New York: Bantam Books, 1981.

The American Clock. New York: Viking, 1980; Dramatists' Play Service, 1980. London: Methuen, 1983.

(b) BOOKS OF PROSE FICTION BY ARTHUR MILLER

Focus. New York: Reynal, 1945. London: Gollancz, 1949. Harmondsworth: Penguin, 1978.

The Misfits. New York: Viking; London: Secker & Warburg, 1961 (with the original short story of the same name). Harmondsworth: Penguin, 1961 (without the original short story).

I Don't Need You Any More. New York: Viking; London: Secker & Warburg; Harmondsworth: Penguin, 1967.

(c) COLLECTIONS

Collected Plays, 1957. See under (a) above.

Collected Plays. Volume Two, 1981. See under (a) above.

The Portable Arthur Miller, edited, with an Introduction, by Harold Clurman. New York: Viking, 1971. Contains *Death of a Salesman, The Crucible, Incident at Vichy, The Price, The Misfits* (two versions), two short stories, a poem, and an extract from *In Russia* (published with Ingeborg Morath, 1969).

The Theater Essays of Arthur Miller, edited by Robert Martin. New York: Viking, 1978. Harmondsworth: Penguin, 1978.

(d) BOOKS ON ARTHUR MILLER

Dennis Welland, *Arthur Miller*. Edinburgh and London: Oliver & Boyd; New York: Grove (Writers and Critics Series), 1961.

Robert Hogan, *Arthur Miller*. Minneapolis, Minn.: University of Minnesota Press (University of Minnesota Pamphlets on American Writers), 1964.

Sheila Huftel, *Arthur Miller: The Burning Glass*. New York: Citadel, 1965.

Leonard Moss, *Arthur Miller*. New York: Twayne (Twayne's United States Authors Series), 1967.

Edward Murray: *Arthur Miller, Dramatist*. New York: Frederick Ungar, 1967.

Robert W. Corrigan (ed.), *Arthur Miller: A Collection of Critical Essays*. Englewood Cliffs, N.J.: Prentice-Hall (Twentieth-century Views Series), 1969.

Richard I. Evans and Arthur Miller, *Psychology and Arthur Miller* (dialogues). New York: Dutton, 1969.

Benjamin Nelson, *Arthur Miller: Portrait of a Playwright*. London: Peter Owen, 1970.

Ronald Hayman, *Arthur Miller*. New York: Frederick Ungar, 1972.

Dennis Welland, *Miller: A Study of His Plays*. London: Eyre Methuen (Modern Theatre Profiles Series), 1979.

Robert A. Martin (ed.), *Arthur Miller: New Perspectives*. Englewood Cliffs, N.J. and London: Prentice-Hall (Twentieth-Century Views Series), 1982.

Neil Carson, *Arthur Miller*. London: Macmillan (Modern Dramatists Series), 1982.

(e) BIBLIOGRAPHY

Tetsumaro Hayashi, 'Arthur Miller: The Dimension of his Art: a Checklist of his Published Works' in *The Serif* (Kent, Ohio) 1967.

Tetsumaro Hayashi: *Arthur Miller Criticism (1930-1967)*. Metuchen, N.J.: Scarecrow Press, 1969.

Index